Full-Service Radio

ELECTRONIC MEDIA GUIDES

Elizabeth Czech-Beckerman *Managing Electronic Media*

Ken Dancyger *Broadcast Writing: Dramas, Comedies, and Documentaries*

Donna L. Halper *Full-Service Radio: Programming for the Community*

Donna L. Halper *Radio Music Directing*

William Hawes *Television Performing: News and Information*

Robert L. Hilliard *The Federal Communications Commission: A Primer*

John R. Hitchcock *Sportscasting*

Andrew F. Inglis *Satellite Technology: An Introduction*

Carla B. Johnston *Election Coverage: Blueprint for Broadcasters*

Marilyn J. Matelski *TV News Ethics*

Marilyn J. Matelski *Daytime Television Programming*

Robert B. Musburger *Electronic News Gathering: A Guide to ENG*

Full-Service Radio
Programming
for the Community

Donna L. Halper

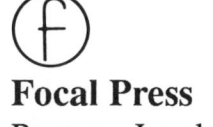
Focal Press
Boston   London

I dedicate this book to the memory of Bob DeLancey, a great teacher and my first real friend; to Neil Mahoney, who encouraged me when I needed it most; to my father and sister, Sam and Judy Halper, who certainly deserve to have a book dedicated to them; to Jon Jacobik, who is the best of all possible husbands; and to the memory of my mother, Bea Halper, who loved books and taught me to do the same.

Focal Press is an imprint of Butterworth–Heinemann.

Copyright © 1991 by Butterworth–Heinemann, a division of Reed Publishing (USA) Inc.
All rights reserved.

No part of this publication may be reproduced, stored in a retrieval system, or transmitted, in any form or by any means, electronic, mechanical, photocopying, recording, or otherwise, without the prior written permission of the publisher.

Recognizing the importance of preserving what has been written, it is the policy of Butterworth Publishers to have the books it publishes printed on acid-free paper, and we exert our best efforts to that end.

Library of Congress Cataloging-in-Publication Data
Halper, Donna L.
Full-service radio: programming for the community / by Donna L. Halper
p. cm.—(Electronic media guide)
Includes bibliographical references.
ISBN 0-240-80083-4
1. Radio broadcasting—United States. I. Title. II. Series
PN1991.3.U6H27   1991
384.54'0973—dc20   90–35778
                                                                   CIP

British Library Cataloguing in Publication Data
Halper, Donna
    Full-service radio: programming for the community.—(Electronic media guide)
    1. Radio services
    I. Title. II. Series
    384.54
    ISBN 0-240-80083-4

Butterworth–Heinemann
80 Montvale Avenue
Stoneham, MA 02180

10 9 8 7 6 5 4 3 2 1

Printed in the United States of America

Contents

Preface   vii
1 From the Beginning   1
2 Radio Programming Matures   8
3 Full-Service and Radio's Golden Age   16
4 Full-Service as a Format   26
5 Full-Service Meets the Challenge   35
6 Full-Service Adapts to the Future   46
7 How To Do Full-Service: The Right Research   58
8 How To Do Full-Service: The Right Programming   71
9 Some Do's and Don'ts in Today's Full-Service   93
Bibliography   101

Preface

Radio has always fascinated me. I've been an active listener since I was little. I knew all the words to the songs, called in for requests, and dreamed that one day I too would be on my favorite station, playing the hits. I was also a sports fan, at a time when most girls weren't, and radio allowed me to hear the important games—I can recall many times when I would sneak my transistor radio into school, hoping the teacher wouldn't notice.

For me, radio was an education. Yes, often I just wanted to hear a hit song, but just as often, I wanted to hear what was happening in other cities. Like many radio fans, I took up DX-ing, listening to distant AM stations. Thanks to CKAC in Montreal (which sounded like 'say-ker-ah-say' to my ear), I improved my French, and learned to say "he shoots, he scores!" and other useful phrases. I heard the Orioles baseball games on WBAL in Baltimore. From WWVA in Wheeling, I received my introduction to Country music, which I might not have done otherwise, since Country was never very popular in Boston. I also heard news from all over the United States, and songs that were never hits in the East but were huge in the South and Midwest. During that time, my "North American Radio-TV Station Guide" listed seven pages of FM stations (I didn't have an FM, but that was okay because we all knew that FM was for classical and educational programming), and over 20 pages of AMs to seek out. Radio listening was an adventure, and I loved it.

My first career goal was to become a sportswriter, but Boston in the 1950s and early 60s was very conservative, and I was told girls couldn't do that. I was also told to forget about becoming a disc jockey, but I wasn't willing to give that one up; in 1968, my dream finally came true. Since then, I've continued to learn about radio, and I enjoy listening to a variety of formats. This book is a study of an important and unique format, a style of radio that is called *Full-Service*. This style features lots of news, sports, local information, and public service, along with some music. My parents introduced me to it back when I was too young to appreciate just how much skill goes into doing the format well. All I knew when I was a kid was that my parents relied on one certain station, especially if bad weather were coming or school might be closed. Years later, while I must admit I am still a rock fan, I've developed great respect for Full-Service radio. In fact, since I became a consultant, Full-Service has been a great resource for me: when I'm in a new city, Full-Service helps me become more familiar with local issues and community leaders.

In this book, you will learn how Full-Service evolved, and why it has outlasted such potential problems as the decline of AM and the ups and downs of the economy.

I hope you enjoy reading it as much as I enjoyed writing it: it was very exciting for me to talk to some of the people I used to listen to when I was DX-ing during my teen years. I'm glad I can pay tribute to some influential stations and share their achievements with you.

Thanks to Focal Press for agreeing with me that the story of Full-Service deserves to be told. Thanks also to the many stations who gave me their time. Space doesn't permit naming them all, but a few who really went out of their way for me were KMOX, KDKA, WMT, WHO, KMA, WJR, CKAC, and WSB. Also, a few excellent libraries helped me out greatly, including the nice folks at Curry College's Levin Library; the Charlotte Public Library; Atlanta-Fulton Public Library; Metropolitan Toronto Reference Library; Allen County Public Library (Fort Wayne); Minneapolis Public Library; and the City Library (Salt Lake City).

Finally, my eternal gratitude to God, without Whom this book could never have been written.

1
From the Beginning

Few listeners today realize that the very first radio format was probably Full-Service. True, the concept of *format* wasn't a part of radio's formative years, nor was anyone concerned with ratings or demographics, but a close look at the history of commercial radio shows that the roots of Full-Service can be traced all the way back to the early 1900s.

Most students of broadcasting know about the achievements of Reginald Fessenden, the professor of electrical engineering at the University of Pittsburgh who was the first to transmit voice over Marconi's amazing invention, the wireless. One of Fessenden's first challenges had been given to him in 1900 by the United States Department of Agriculture; the Weather Service wanted to explore sending weather information to the many ships at sea. However, Fessenden's goal was to move beyond Morse code transmissions. On December 24, 1906, he finally succeeded: wireless operators in ships off the East Coast suddenly found themselves listening to a woman singing, a violin solo, and a brief talk. The quality of the reception was poor, but Fessenden had now proved such broadcasts were possible.

Meanwhile, amateur radio hobbyists began trying to improve upon Fessenden's work. One enterprising gentleman in San Jose was able to broadcast music and advertising as early as 1914; unfortunately, to do so, he illegally tapped into the power lines of the Santa Fe Railway, which obviously was not amused. Other more legal radio pioneers included Lee DeForest, who saw radio as a medium that would bring culture into the average person's home. An opera lover, he wanted everyone to be able to hear this music, not just those who could afford to buy tickets. With this in mind, he built a 125-foot tower on the roof of his factory so that he could broadcast half-hour concerts of phonograph music each night.

Amateur radio stations were quickly springing up all over the United States; what had at first been dismissed as a fad expanded to the point where by 1916, there were over 10,000 licensed amateur radio stations. Then the rapid growth of amateur radio, and the great interest in further expanding the uses of radio, came to an abrupt halt as a result of World War I; in 1917, the United States government shut down all amateur stations for security reasons, and the navy took control of how and when radio would be used. Now the war effort came to depend on radio to transmit vital information to ships; radio also proved good for morale, as the navy found out when it began broadcasting a program of news from various U.S. cities so that the troops could catch up on what was going on back home. Suddenly, radio wasn't the domain of the inventor or the hobbyist: it was a business, and both the military and the government saw the potential.

In 1918, attempts were made to pass legislation that would permanently put radio under the navy's control, but public sentiment was opposed to such a move; after the war ended, interest in radio was as strong as before, and all the amateurs were patiently waiting to get back on the air. They lobbied their representatives furiously when they heard about the proposed law, and their vehement opposition (along with some old-fashioned politics—the Republicans in Congress took the opportunity to castigate the Democrats for encroaching upon private industry) doomed the measure. The amateur radio operators and their stations returned, and with them also returned the eagerness to experiment with voice and music.

Another of radio's pioneers, Frank Conrad, had such a successful amateur station that he frequently received fan mail and song requests from other amateurs who heard his broadcasts. Since radio had now moved far away from Morse code, amateurs were able to introduce their families to it, and listening and talking with people from distant cities became an enjoyable way to pass an evening. The more people were attracted to radio, the more they needed receivers: busy Americans lacked the time or the talent to build their own, which led several major companies to increase production to keep up with the sudden demand. It is doubtful that these companies ever imagined that by 1922, sales of radio sets and parts would total $60 million.

The many amateur and experimental stations of 1900 to 1918 paved the way for broadcasts aimed at a wider audience. The station which did this first is open to some debate: in the United States, it is widely accepted that KDKA's broadcast of the Harding-Cox presidential election returns on November 2, 1920, was the trailblazer. However, Canadians point to an equally important date, 6 months earlier. On May 20, station XWA in Montreal (later CFCF, "*Canada's First*") broadcast the music of an orchestra and a soloist; the performance was heard clearly in Ottawa, over 100 miles away, and was enjoyed by such dignitaries as the governor-general and the prime minister. Neither XWA nor KDKA had much power—KDKA had only 100 watts.

Although radio receivers were becoming more popular, still it was estimated at the time of KDKA's broadcast that fewer than 1000 receivers were in homes. Yet both stations earned great respect for their "firsts," as they demonstrated conclusively how radio could deliver a major event with more immediacy than any other medium, and it was potentially available to vast numbers of people. Once this point was made, there was no stopping radio's growth.

In early 1921, XWA was still the only station in all of Canada and KDKA was one of only ten in the entire United States. By the end of 1922, however, Americans could choose from 564 stations, and Canadians in western cities like Vancouver and Calgary could hear what had caused all that excitement in Ottawa; also, French-Canadians got their first outlet, CKAC in Montreal. It didn't take long for radio to become accepted as an essential source of entertainment and information. In their book *Border Radio,* authors Bill Crawford and Gene Fowler speak of the great impact radio had on the society.

> It is difficult for our video-glutted generation to imagine what radio meant to Americans in the 1920's. Radio was the housewife's companion, the friendly voice of consolation that brightened the world of cooking, washing and child-rearing with music, romance and understanding conversation. Radio became the center of . . . family entertainment as children, parents and grandparents gathered . . . in the radio room and marvelled at the sounds transported mysteriously from faraway lands. Radio was hailed as the world's greatest source of knowledge . . . the invention that would stop all wars.

Of course, radio never became the panacea its earliest fans expected, but that doesn't diminish how it changed people's lives. For one thing, it eliminated some class distinctions: as Lee DeForest had hoped, now any person, rich or poor, could have equal access to opera, presidential speeches, or whatever. Also, listeners had a choice—if they didn't like a program, they could tune the dial to another station or simply turn off the radio. As radio expanded and began offering a wider variety of programming, listeners in the privacy and comfort of their homes could hear about (and sometimes from) the biggest celebrities of the day, from politicians to sports greats, movie stars to poets, jazz singers to famous philanthropists. All that any interested person needed was the proper equipment; radio did the rest.

Most new inventions have their pluses and minuses, and although radio seemed more a plus than most, it did have its detractors. Some critics worried that radio was too much of a solitary activity and might keep people from socializing. This seemed a needless worry given that early stations did not broadcast for 24 (or even 12) hours a day; KDKA only broadcast for one hour each evening in its first months. WTIC in Hartford broadcast from 7:45 to 10:24 P.M. its first evening. Although some early stations tried to keep some sort of regular schedule, many did not—they just broadcast until they ran out of material. Meanwhile, other critics debated what radio's proper role should be, expressing a belief that radio should educate not entertain. Several journalists of the early 1920s wrote that radio should be used as a way to make average Americans more cultured, by playing "good music" (opera) as opposed to "popular music" (jazz). Given that this debate still goes on even today, except that now critics lament the lack of classical music and the popularity of rock, it seems the more things change, the more they stay the same.

In those exciting, experimental early days, radio programming had an almost "anything-goes" attitude. The positive side of this was it enabled stations to devote much-needed attention to local issues; several Iowa stations, for example, became experts on matters crucial to the many farmers in their listening audience. Radio also brought church services to the homes of shut-ins and provided a forum for politicians and local business leaders. Since radio was still new (and phonograph records were not always in great enough supply, nor did they always have the sound quality radio needed), it often needed live performers. This brought many soon-to-be-famous people their first big break.

However, there was also a negative side to radio's seeming willingness to try anything: as a result, the caliber of the programs varied widely. For every virtuoso, there was an Aunt Em playing her kazoo off-key. For every great orator, there was some would-be poet with forgettable verses. Most bothersome of all, for every honest local business leader, there was a charlatan extolling the virtue of an unproven (and possibly dangerous) "miracle drug" guaranteed to cure any illness a gullible listener might have. There was no consistency and no way of knowing what to expect from many of the new stations. Few listeners really objected, however, because radio was still a source of wonderment, and its many fans forgave the frequent technical problems and the strange programming decisions.

There was one group that wasn't so tolerant of radio's early excesses, and it was made up of certain members of Congress. Led by then–Secretary of Commerce (and later President) Herbert Hoover, these people were concerned about the proliferation of commercials on radio. Hoover even stated that commercial advertising would ruin radio, and he wanted to ban commercials entirely. Granted, some listeners had found out the hard way that a "miracle drug" wasn't such a miracle after all, but the majority of the audience found commercials useful: now they could learn about new products or find out who had a sale. Radio certainly had a beneficial effect on the local economy; it helped neighborhood merchants to become better-known and compete with chain stores.

What really made Hoover's view unpopular was that most of the early stations were owned by large companies, who saw radio as an ideal way to promote their own products and services. Many newspapers (who didn't yet regard radio as competition) owned stations, as did department stores and manufacturers of radio receivers. In Canada, even the National Railways owned radio stations. Some stations just used whatever call letters the Department of Commerce had arbitrarily assigned them (KDKA was not the initials of anyone), while other stations obtained call letters that advertised who owned them. Thus, WTIC in Hartford stood for *T*ravelers *I*nsurance *C*ompany; WOC in Davenport, Iowa, spoke for the Palmer School of Chiropractic ("*W*orld *o*f *C*hiropractic"); from Sears' advertising slogan emerged WLS in Chicago ("*W*orld's *L*argest *S*tore"); and across town, WGN evoked the slogan of its parent company, the *Chicago Tribune* ("*W*orld's *G*reatest *N*ewspaper"). Seeing little popular support, Hoover ultimately abandoned his efforts to keep commercials off the air.

Ironically, stations themselves were reticent to accept advertising at first, preferring to only promote the products of their owners. Some stations didn't even want to go that far: when WSB in Atlanta first appeared, on March 16, 1922, an article in the *Atlanta Journal* (which owned the station) stated that WSB would be operated by the newspaper "purely for the benefit and enjoyment of the public, and there will be no commercial feature connected with it." That soon proved to be a minority view, as WEAF in New York (owned by A T & T) became the first station to officially air commercials (the first one cost $50 and lasted a full 10 minutes) in mid-1922, and many other stations quickly saw the advantage of forging strong ties with the local business community. This positive attitude toward business, which even went so far as to make heroes out of local industry leaders, remains an important part of what we call Full-Service radio today. The precedent was set by some resourceful owners of the 1920s, men and women who realized that it made good sense to be a booster of local businesses and their achievements. Thus, radio stations were able to give even the smallest towns a feeling of pride in their communities, and radio became a focal point for news about local people and local events.

If KDKA's broadcast of election returns in late 1920 was a milestone in the history of radio programming, it was also a milestone in the evolution of Full-Service. Years later, when specialized formats ruled, Full-Service would remain true to the original vision of radio's pioneers: to keep listeners *both* entertained and informed.

The next step in this process occurred in 1921, and again, KDKA was first. The introduction of sports programming brought another dimension to radio's usefulness. KDKA's initial sports broadcast was a local boxing match, with commentary done by a Pittsburgh sportswriter. KDKA soon had its own staff announcer, Harold Arlin, doing play-by-play for the Pittsburgh Pirates baseball games, and the station built a reputation for extensive coverage of local sports.

It was David Sarnoff though who capitalized on sports programming. Sarnoff had always believed in radio, and when he became general manager of Radio Corporation of America (RCA), he saw a chance to show doubters what radio could do. He also saw a great opportunity to go one-up on a major competitor: Westinghouse, which owned KDKA, was in fierce competition with RCA for control of the now-lucrative home receiver market. On July 2, Sarnoff got permission to put a station on the air for 1 day (WJY) in order to broadcast the biggest sporting event of that time—the championship fight between Dempsey and Carpenter. The boxing fans of New York were happy about this, but what made the event unique was a specially arranged hookup of loudspeakers and receivers in several different cities. This transformed the fight from a local broadcast to one that was heard by an estimated 300,000 fans from New York to Florida.

Not to be outdone by RCA, Westinghouse had its Newark station, WJZ, broadcast a game of the World Series in October and received thousands of letters praising WJZ (later WABC) for bringing the game to the many fans who had been unable to obtain tickets.

Although educators kept writing articles about how radio was not devoting enough time to culture, the public was delighted that the new medium was so enjoyable. The rivalry between companies like RCA and Westinghouse made radio even more enjoyable, because every time a new event (sports, politics, or otherwise) was about to occur, stations fought to put it on the air first. Another positive result of this was that radio receivers were now an indispensable part of life. By 1924, Christmas gift catalogues were listing 16 different brands, all claiming to be superior. David Sarnoff's faith in radio was richly rewarded: from 1922 to 1924, RCA sold $83.5 million worth of radio receivers.

It is doubtful that the Department of Commerce, which had been licensing radio stations in the early 20s, had any idea how quickly radio would spread. This lack of foresight caused numerous problems. Although there were some regulations that stations had to obey, they had been formulated in 1912, at a time when commercial radio didn't yet exist. These rules didn't adequately relate to an industry that was now turning regular profits from advertising (in 1923, WEAF made $150,000 for its owner, A T & T), nor did they address an industry that by 1927 had 732 stations.

Never anticipating radio's incredible growth, the Department of Commerce had simply assigned all low-powered stations to the same general area of the AM dial. This was fine when there were only ten stations, but soon the dial was so cluttered that stations were forced to share the same frequency even during the same day: one would broadcast for a few hours, then another, then a third, and so on. Some stations used the frequency only during the day and others only at night. To make matters worse, some owners didn't like their dial position, so they began moving around, to the great confusion of the audience. If that weren't enough, some stations would raise their power at whim, especially if a new competitor were coming to town. This made life miserable for Canadian stations, many of which would find themselves drowned out by yet another American station boosting its power.

The AM band was chaotic, and stations were too numerous to be supervised by an agency as busy as the Department of Commerce. Thus, in 1927, a new agency was created, and its sole task was to oversee radio: the Federal Radio Commission (FRC) also came with a new piece of legislation, the Radio Act of 1927. Its critics accused it of favoring stations owned by major corporations at the expense of small and/or educational stations, but even if it had its flaws, the Radio Act was a badly needed beginning in the process of bringing order to the AM band and making owners more accountable for what was on their stations.

The Radio Act made it clear that while profits were certainly desirable, they were not the only reason for having a license. Radio stations were now expected to operate "in the public interest, convenience or necessity." This was not a new idea; astute owners had always run their stations in a responsible manner, even without a law to say they must.

It is not surprising that many of the stations of the 1920s which devoted themselves to being a positive force in their market are around today, still making a positive impact. Some of them have even become perfect examples of everything good Full-Service radio stands for. KDKA, for example, issued this amazingly modern-sounding statement of purpose when it went on the air in 1920: "To work hand in hand with the press; to provide programs of interest and benefit to the greatest number; to avoid monotony; to assign distinctive features regular times for the convenience of the listener; and to operate a daily service of regularly scheduled programs." This credo was echoed by other now-legendary Full-Service stations. When Travelers Insurance Vice President Walter Cowles signed WTIC on the air in 1925, his opening remarks pledged to "earn the goodwill, friendship and confidence of those who hear us." The forerunners of today's Full-Service are too numerous to mention, but they certainly include KDKA, WTIC, WCCO, KMOX, WLW, WBZ, KMA, WMT, WGY, WOWO, WJR, WHO, KSL, WSB, and in Canada, CKAC, CFRB, and CBL.

Although some owners got into radio when it was still easy to do so, made some money, and then got right out, stations like these pioneers became known for their excellent reputation and commitment to the community. We will profile some of them and discuss their success in more detail later, but for now, suffice it to say that without their hard work, there would be no Full-Service radio today.

2 ▼ Radio Programming Matures

By contemporary standards, radio programming in the mid-20s could still sound amateurish. There were persistent technical problems—signals that faded in and out, and microphones that refused to work reliably. Then there was "studio fright." Stage performers were not yet accustomed to radio, and when they arrived at the studio, they panicked. Sometimes it wasn't their fault, however: early stations looked rather intimidating to anyone who wasn't an engineer.

One journalist described his first impressions of WSB in Atlanta, when it went on the air in March of 1922, from the fifth floor of the Atlanta Journal Building: he noted that the room WSB used was a maze of tangled wires, batteries, dials, tubes, generators, a few folding chairs for the announcers, and ominous signs that read "Danger," "High Voltage," and "Quiet Zone."

The idea of comfortable studios was still unknown. WJZ first broadcast from the roof of the Westinghouse plant in Newark; the only way to get up there was to climb an iron ladder and crawl through a hatchway. It was no wonder performers were reticent to be on the air. The famous comedian Ed Wynn was so upset at telling his best jokes to a silent, empty room that he demanded an audience. WJZ obliged him by rounding up all the telephone operators, cleaning people, and electricians they could find working in the vicinity, and in February of 1922, the first studio audience was born. Even with a studio audience though (and not all stations had them in those early days), radio could make a performer uneasy. Stations dealt with this in some ingenious ways, including disguising the microphone as a lamp or putting plants around it to conceal its presence.

As it became obvious that radio was popular, stations improved upon their studios. KDKA had also begun on a rooftop (as had many stations of that time, including KSL in Salt Lake City). Others began in garages (WJAM, later WMT in Cedar Rapids, Iowa) or even in the station manager's living room (WOWO in Fort Wayne, Indiana). It wasn't long before KDKA had progressed from a rooftop shack to a tent to studios in the William Penn Hotel. WCCO in Minneapolis also found a new home in a hotel, The Nicollet; its previous incarnation, WLAG had broadcast from the Oak Grove Hotel. Having studios in a hotel enabled stations to be more visible and provide a pleasant environment for anyone who wanted to be a spectator. WJZ, meanwhile, had moved from the roof to a converted coatroom to its own building; its new studios had plush carpets, an expensive piano, and the use of a limousine to transport the performers. WOWO ended up on the second floor of its owners, the Main Auto Supply Company, but it had to share its new studios with WGL, the other station in Fort Wayne. KSL, owned by the Mormon Church (and originally called KZN), moved from the roof of the Deseret News Building to the basement of the Vermont Building, which it soon outgrew, causing several more moves to bigger and better locations. WTIC in Hartford had studios that reflected the elegance of the era: mahogany microphone stands, blue velvet drapes, and, even before studio audiences, announcers who were expected to dress formally, in tuxedos and evening gowns.

As the idea of having nice studios took hold, so did the idea of making radio more responsive to the public. One way to do this was with remote broadcasts. Again, KDKA got there first, in January 1921, when the station broadcast the Sunday service live from Calvary Episcopal Church. As it became obvious that radio could go right to the audience, stations began finding new ways to do remotes. Two competitors in Shenandoah, Iowa (KFNF and KMA) each built concert halls and then tried to outdo the other with stage shows, square dances, and other live broadcasts; people who attended were given free food and, sometimes, prizes. KMA's auditorium seated 1000, was designed like a Moorish garden, and could show motion pictures whenever KMA wasn't using it for live broadcasts.

Meanwhile, in Canada, the Canadian National Railways had found an interesting variation on remotes: CNR sent broadcasts to some of their moving trains. They even equipped certain trains with a special parlor car, complete with a radio receiver and a uniformed attendant. CNR later used this creative approach at the stations they owned. They broadcast original plays as early as 1925 and offered programming in both French and English. They also aired opera, folk music, and shows about current events, and managed to link up their stations from Ottawa to Vancouver in a type of network.

The idea of networks was still experimental in the early 1920s. One of the first successful examples in the United States occurred in 1923 when WEAF in New York joined WNAC in Boston to broadcast a football game; this would be repeated from Canada to Boston when CKAC in Montreal linked up with WBZ to broadcast hockey in 1925. Westinghouse stations like KDKA, WJZ, and KYW linked with General Electric's Schenectady, New York station WGY for some programs, as networking slowly expanded.

In 1926, A T & T sold WEAF for $1 million to RCA, and the station became the flagship of David Sarnoff's newest creation, the National Broadcasting Company (NBC) in November of that year. Sarnoff saw NBC as a way to offer entertainment coast to coast, and it wasn't long before listeners all over the country heard the Rose Bowl.

Soon after, in 1927, William Paley started the Columbia Broadcasting System (CBS). Networks were a major help to local stations: they filled up the broadcast day, offering listeners the chance to hear the most famous singers, comedians, and dance bands. Even CKAC briefly affiliated with a U.S. network (CBS) for that very reason. The networks also became a forum for presidents to get their messages to the widest possible audience: during the Depression, President Roosevelt used radio 20 times in 9 months.

The Radio Act of 1927 had addressed some of radio's problems. Stations no longer jumped around the dial the way they once did. As radio ceased to be new, audiences and sponsors began having greater expectations for it. Although KDKA had promised to have a set schedule, many stations in the mid-20s still didn't; Aunt Em and her kazoo gradually were replaced, and stations sought a more consistent style. Most stations had their own orchestras or in-house musicians. Many by now had a regular group of guest speakers, but programming was still an adventure. Sometimes the guests were delayed; sometimes they decided they didn't want to appear after all.

Tommy Cowan, the first full-time announcer in New York (on WJZ) was not only expected to read the weather, do the sign-on and sign-off, and give the time; he was also the talent scout for WJZ, persuading performers to make the long trip to WJZ's first studios in Newark. If he couldn't get any performers, he was expected to fill up the time himself. To do this, he once had to convince Thomas Edison to lend him a phonograph (WJZ didn't have one of its own when it first went on the air). Edison, it turned out, didn't like the way records sounded on radio, so he demanded his phonograph back; this prompted Westinghouse to finally buy some records and a phonograph of its own.

Meanwhile, Tommy Cowan was becoming quite popular, which was amazing given the fact that he was broadcasting at a time when announcers were not allowed to use their names. Taking a tradition from the wireless days, the announcers identified themselves only by initials. Cowan was ACN—A for announcer, C for Cowan, and N for Newark (later New York). The owners liked this; they feared that if announcers became too well-known, they would demand more money. (Announcing in the early 1920s was not yet a lucrative position. Announcers may have been asked to dress elegantly and speak with flawless diction, but most were paid about $45 a week and were not yet treated like celebrities, the way some are today.)

Even with the disappearance of some of the truly amateurish shows, radio programming in the 20s was still developing. Much of what was on the air was very much geared to the local audience, in a style we know today as *block programming*—blocks of time were devoted to a particular theme, and there wasn't always a common thread to hold the entire broadcast day together.

In Iowa, which had been a hotbed of radio from the beginning (in 1926, this state alone had *20* stations), KFNF in Shenandoah achieved great success as "The Friendly Farmer Station." KFNF featured daily talks by experts who spoke on gardening, planting, agriculture, and the raising of animals; these experts answered questions and provided useful information. Just when it seemed as if KFNF was an educational station, there were musical selections from groups like the Cornfield Canaries and the Seedhouse Girls. There was also a "Letters to Henry" show wherein station owner Henry Field of the Henry Field Seed Company answered his mail on the air. Then there were the church services, fiddling contests, and everything a listener could ever want to know about how to keep baby chicks healthy.

Seeing how well KFNF was doing, Earl May of the Earl May Seed & Nursery Company put KMA on the air in 1925 to give some new competition. Both stations had 500 watts, and both used some of the same local musicians, but KMA was determined to carve out its own niche. It addition to building its elegant auditorium (KFNF had one too), KMA became known for the pancakes and sausages station personnel fed to everyone who attended the station's live broadcasts.

KMA's positioning strategy was to one-up KFNF. KMA tried to offer more famous entertainers and bigger and better experts, as well as more helpful tips about gardening and farming, a show for children, baseball scores, and more news—local as well as national. KMA also offered the talents of May's Mandolin Musicians, the How-Do-You-Do Boys, and the Delmonico Hotel Orchestra. Then there were the contests, such as the one where a woman sat at a typewriter in the studio and the at-home audience had to guess by listening to the sound of the keys exactly how many words she typed. KMA also had testimonial shows about the joys of life in Shenandoah, and, of course, commercials for the latest seed catalog. Both KMA and KFNF did so well that musicians would often perform for free, just to get valuable exposure. Farmers expressed their pleasure at having access to so much up-to-date information, presented in such an entertaining manner.

If Shenandoah had room for more than one successful station, other much larger cities could too, and stations in these cities kept searching for the way to their listeners' hearts. Clearly, what made Iowa farmers happy might not necessarily work elsewhere, so stations sought programs that would be unique to their market. Westinghouse's KYW in Chicago went on the air in 1921 as an all-opera station. Every day, KYW broadcast the entire program of the Chicago Civic Opera Company. Despite the poor reception quality of early radio sets, these broadcasts were very successful. There were several reasons for this, one being that radio was still new and almost anything it offered generated excitement. Just as important to music lovers, however, was this: until now, unless a person had tickets to the opera, there was no other way to enjoy live music. Phonograph records could only hold a 4- to 5-minute selection, which meant that an entire opera on record would have to be interrupted every few minutes while the disk was changed. Thanks to radio, music lovers could now hear long selections by the most famous performers, with no unwanted pauses in the middle. This became a major selling point as radio reception continued to improve.

Opera wasn't a magic programming answer either. WTIC in Hartford had a different approach: vaudeville. Thanks to the resources of their parent company, Travelers Insurance, WTIC had already acquired an excellent symphony orchestra; in fact, a series of programs on music appreciation earned the station critical acclaim and led to a similar series that NBC broadcast. WTIC had its own string quartet and a dance band. The station also did remotes from hotels and clubs all over greater Hartford. These remote broadcasts were so successful that station management was encouraged to take them beyond the usual glee club and piano recitals. Since famous entertainers were appearing on stage at the Capitol Theater, WTIC decided to broadcast their performances live. WTIC became the first station to present such legendary stars as Jack Benny, Edgar Bergen and Charlie McCarthy.

The station also interviewed bandleader John Philip Sousa, but he refused to play. WTIC even interviewed the great Houdini. As if all these big stars weren't enough to keep the audience entertained, WTIC even did one show from a moving aircraft: the governor of Connecticut loved to fly, so he flew over Hartford while speaking into a shortwave radio, at which time, WTIC picked up the signal and rebroadcast it. Like KMA with its lavish auditorium, WTIC knew that making people remember the station was the key to popularity, and whether it was a live interview with a major celebrity or a broadcast from a plane, WTIC was committed to doing creative and exciting radio shows.

As competition increased, stations were eager to find ways to distinguish themselves in the listener's mind; after all, if a station sounded like all the others, why would anyone choose it? Radio in the 1920s was not driven by Arbitron or Birch; it was, however, driven by the audience, which tended to be very vocal about likes and dislikes. Advertisers too weren't shy about letting a station know their opinions. So radio executives continued to provide the audience with more good reasons to listen.

Not every station had an airplane. Some stations made their mark just by being dependable. One of these was WOC in Davenport, started in 1921 by Dr. B. J. Palmer. In addition to being president of the Palmer School of Chiropractic, Palmer was also a world traveler and a published author before his involvement with WOC. One day, after a market report started late, he installed a large clock in the studio and instructed the announcers to begin every show with the correct time. Soon, despite having only 50 watts, WOC became the station listeners could set their watch to, and time checks had become part of WOC's success.

Later, Palmer bought WHO in Des Moines, an already respected station thanks to its in-depth farm news. Many other stations, including KDKA and KMA, had broadcast some farm news, but WHO's Farm Department offered such extensive coverage and made such a positive impact in the community that it would be frequently emulated in the years ahead. WHO (so named at a time when listeners were wondering "Who is this?" and "Who are we listening to?") had the benefit of being one of the few 50,000-watt stations, giving it even wider listenership. This certainly helped WHO's sports announcer get good exposure: his name was Ronald "Dutch" Reagan.

While Ronald Reagan was doing play by play in the early 1930s, WLW in Cincinnati was enjoying the permission it received to have *500,000 watts*. Permission was rescinded in 1939, but during those years, surveys showed WLW, which called itself "The Nation's Station," was number one in 13 states! WLW also became known as the "Cradle of the Stars" from all the celebrities who performed live at its studios. Like WTIC, WLW saw that presenting big-name entertainers would attract more listeners. WLW had many big names: actor Roy Rogers, jazz great "Fats" Waller, comedian Red Skelton, sportscaster extraordinaire Red Barber, and more. WLW soon became a source of network programs.

Sometimes good musicians weren't available, and some stations turned to radio drama as an alternative. Early shows were primitive: only one microphone and no sound effects. Through trial and error, these presentations were rewritten and adapted especially for radio. Some were derived from already well-known sources: two examples of this ran on NBC in the late 20s, "Great Moments in History" and "Biblical Dramas." Listeners seemed to find them interesting enough, but they were a far cry from what we would consider drama—they were more like a parent reading a story to a child. Some local dramatic groups had distinguished themselves as early as 1922. When WGY in Schenectady, New York, found a lack of good musicians, they turned to dramatic presentations. The WGY Players did so well that by 1924, they were doing network performances. CBS had a successful continuing series in 1928—"True Story," based on articles from the popular crime magazine. However, the one show that would firmly establish radio as *the* entertainment medium was a 15-minute comedy program whose roots were in Chicago. It was originally called "Sam 'n' Henry" when it began airing on WGN in 1926, and it developed a large local following. Since WGN didn't want to syndicate it, the two men who had created and voiced it, Freeman Gosden and Charles Correll, moved over to WMAQ, where they changed the show's name to "Amos 'n' Andy." By August of 1929, NBC had picked it up, and a nationwide craze had begun. So popular was the show in its heyday that an estimated 40 million people (including President Coolidge) stopped whatever they were doing to listen. Although "Amos 'n' Andy" seems somewhat racist by today's standards, the characters were portrayed so well and the situations they found themselves in were so universal that the program had great appeal. It also made sponsors happy: Pepsodent, which sponsored it first, noticed an immediate jump in sales. So did the makers of radios, as even in the midst of the Depression, people had to get a radio to hear the next "Amos 'n' Andy" episode. No program prior to this had such an impact on so many people in so many different parts of the country.

In addition to comedies like "Amos 'n' Andy" and one other ethnic-based show, "The Goldbergs," radio serials appeared. These "soap operas" had been tried with limited success in the late 1920s, but they really became popular in the early 30s. Undoubtedly, the Depression played a part in this: with so many Americans suffering, movies (for those who could afford them) and radio shows helped people to forget their problems for a while. Although the broadcast day was still expanding, even by 1930 few stations were on the air for more than 14 hours a day. Owners still believed, for example, that there weren't enough people available to warrant doing a morning show; some stations thus signed on at 11 A.M. Mid-afternoons were also considered unimportant, until changes in the society became so obvious that stations adjusted to them. Soap operas became an eagerly awaited form of escapist entertainment: critics deplored them, but women (and many men too) listened faithfully to the trials and tribulations of such heroines as "Ma Perkins," "Helen Trent" and "Our Gal Sunday." It was sin, scandal, and sorrow in 15-minute doses, and it sold a lot of soap for the sponsors.

Another change taking place involved the style of the announcers. During radio's early days, announcers were trained in diction and elocution. Network auditions required reading such phrases as "The seething sea ceaseth, and thus the seething sea sufficeth us." Radio, however, was a medium for the average American, who, it became obvious, wanted entertainers not professors. Stations experimented with hiring vaudeville performers to do radio shows. Two of the first, and most successful, in the 1920s were Billy Jones and Ernie Hare, called "The Happiness Boys" because they were sponsored by the Happiness Candy Stores. Jones and Hare did make people happy; they sang and told incredibly corny jokes on several New York stations. People loved their easygoing, jovial manner. Their success soon led to an almost endless procession of imitators all over the country, proving that even in the 20s, one good idea could beget hundreds of copies.

Gradually, those owners who had doubted it realized there were enough listeners in the mornings, and some interesting experiments took place within this time period. WOR in New York filled the time with exercises, in the belief that people who woke up early must want something healthy (a far cry from the "Morning Zoo" and "Shock-Jock" wake-up shows of the 1980s). One notable experiment took place in Chicago on KYW in 1929, with a unique program that was about 10 years ahead of its time. KYW had long since stopped being the all-opera station; now, in 1929, it offered a morning show called "The Musical Clock," hosted by a woman named Halloween Martin. Ms. Martin gave the time and temperature, read the weather, and played phonograph records; she even took requests and discovered from talking with listeners that they wanted light, up-tempo music in the early morning. Her show was quite popular—she received thousands of fan letters, and the critics said she had a pleasant voice.

WJZ, which had one popular woman announcer (Bertha Brainard) who reviewed plays, took a survey in 1926 and found that its listeners preferred male announcers by an overwhelming margin, but Halloween Martin's morning show was very successful. Still, by the mid-30s, few stations would have women announcers in any role other than the traditional confines of giving recipes or homemaking tips. All that aside, however, the morning hours were finally being treated as important. Also, the owners had been forced to abandon all attempts to keep their announcers anonymous. The listeners wanted to know the names of these people who had become their new friends; and the sponsors wanted to know the announcers, because a popular announcer would make an impact giving testimonials for their products. Morning shows slowly gained acceptance in the early 30s; meanwhile, one New York announcer was beginning to set the standard still used by Full-Service morning shows today. John Gambling started on the air almost by accident: he was an engineer at WOR, and when the host of the exercise program missed a shift, Gambling filled in. The program didn't survive, but Gambling did. His wake-up shows featured a blend of good conversation, interesting guests, weather and time, and just enough music. Eventually, his time period got a name: "Rambling with Gambling," became a major success.

News was another late addition to radio. Before 1930, some local stations sporadically covered a local event: WSB interrupted regular programming one day in 1922 to tell of a fire, and disaster was averted when off-duty fire fighters heard the report and rushed to the scene to help out. WGN, owned by the *Chicago Tribune*, had a daily news program during the early 20s; it was derived from stories in the *Tribune*.

However, most stations covered the big national stories more than the local ones, assuming they carried any news at all. As for the networks, they too devoted little time to news. Sponsors believed people weren't interested in it, so the networks concentrated on entertainment programming, which sponsors liked. Now and then, a network commentator would analyze an important story, but there was nothing that resembled "news on the hour." CBS did have one popular news show: "The March of Time," sponsored by *Time Magazine*, was a weekly dramatization (complete with sound effects) of the past week's top stories.

By 1928, however, many local stations were paying more attention to news. WLW began offering regular 10-minute newscasts that year. WGN expanded its coverage, and stations like WTIC, KDKA, KMA, and WHO were in the process of building strong local news staffs. The networks wouldn't really commit to extensive news until the onset of World War II in the late 30s, so the local stations had an excellent opportunity to shine. To this day, complete local news is an element for which Full-Service is known and respected.

Meanwhile, radio programming in the late 20s made yet another change. Owners were surprised to find they had again underestimated the size of the available audience in another daypart—late evenings. Just how many shift workers and insomniacs there were was admirably demonstrated by Leo Fitzpatrick, "The Merry Old Chief" of WDAF, who invited his listeners to join a mythical society of late-night fans called the "Kansas City Nighthawks." Over two million people wrote in to request a membership card. Soon, there were more late-night announcers, and some had a large following: the best known of the 20s included Lambdin Kay, "The Little Colonel" of WSB, Atlanta; George Hay, "The Solemn Old Judge" of WLS, Chicago; and Harold Hough, "The Hired Hand" of WBAP, Fort Worth.

As late as the early 30s, many stations lacked a consistent music policy and played a variety of music from classical to the day's popular songs. Some stations tried to keep up with changing tastes: as jazz caught on, despite music critics who felt it was vulgar, stations like WMT introduced jazz shows. Also, despite efforts to bring culture to the audience, popular music slowly won out over opera and classical at a majority of stations. In the South, Country music was what the listeners wanted. WSB was probably the first to program Country regularly, in 1922; WBAP broadcast the first radio barn dance (1½ hours of square dance and fiddle tunes) in 1923. WBT, helped by having 50,000 watts, made Charlotte as famous as Nashville. WBT attracted so many major country stars (The Carter Family and Bill Monroe were among the many who performed live) that several record companies set up offices in Charlotte. It became a truism for up-and-coming performers that exposure on WBT could lead to a recording contract. Whether playing Country, jazz, or pop, these stations were paving the way for Full-Service.

3
▼ Full-Service and
▼ Radio's Golden Age

Although the other media had ignored radio during its early days, no one could call it a fad anymore. In fact, now radio was in intense competition with the very newspapers who had purchased stations in the early days. Soon, radio even had magazines of its own, devoted to radio's growing list of personalities and achievements. Most people had at least one radio; many had several. Radio no longer had to fight for its share of attention.

Unfortunately, some of the attention radio was getting was negative, thanks to some of radio's more notorious participants. One was Father Charles Coughlin, whose weekly programs on such otherwise reputable stations as WJR in Detroit and WLW in Cincinnati (and later on CBS itself) turned from religious matters to virulently anti-Jewish tirades. Father Coughlin was an excellent speaker, and his other favorite subjects were denouncing the president and blaming wealthy people for the Depression; he said that if the international bankers weren't stopped, the world would continue to suffer. He presented himself as the one truth-teller, the one person who stood for the average person's rights. With his ability to know which emotional buttons to push and an audience of poor and angry Americans, he soon had his own cult of personality by way of radio: he was on 28 stations and his pleas for donations to fund his cause brought in $500,000 in 1933 alone. He became so powerful that he was able to generate over a million letters from supporters when CBS dropped his program.

Another man with great but undeserved power from his exposure on radio was "Doctor Brinkley," who had really paid a diploma mill $500 for his degree. Brinkley made millions selling phony medicines by mail order to naïve listeners who heard his amazing claims on the station he owned, KFKB in Milford, Kansas. He also performed a dubious surgical procedure using goat glands that was supposed to restore virility. When the American Medical Association challenged both his degree and his claims, he sold his station for $90,000 and headed for Mexico, where he had no trouble getting back on the air, at a 75,000-watt station called XER. This station's strong signal beamed the doctor right back into the United States, and by 1932, he was receiving an average of 27,000 letters a week, proving you can fool some of the people a lot of the time.

There were a few other quacks and demagogues who saw radio as a perfect way to become famous. Also, certain special programs were really blatant propaganda—at that time, there were no official rules about being balanced or objective, so some very biased shows, such as "Forum of Liberty" and "Voice of the Crusaders" were aired with their content unchallenged. These were only a few of the issues which led the FRC to transition into the Federal Communications Commission (FCC) in 1934.

As the Depression worsened, radio's importance grew, as did the power of the networks. Comedy was especially popular, as big names like Jack Benny, George Burns & Gracie Allen, and Ed Wynn did their best to make America smile during difficult times. Although the American economy was in bad shape, radio still made a profit.

Something new had also been added by now: ratings. In 1930, the networks and their sponsors had stopped trying to guess which shows were listened to the most; stations could charge higher rates for their most popular programs. Thus, Crossley, Inc., was hired to do the first ratings, which it did by telephone recall. NBC won these initial ratings wars: their show, "Amos 'n' Andy," was found to be four times as popular as any show on CBS. From then on, ratings would be a regular part of radio; by 1935, Hooper was the company of choice, and radio stations worried about their "Hooperatings."

There were still a few new programming types that arose in the 1930s. One of the best-loved was quiz shows. WTIC claims to have first developed the genre in 1927 with "Jack Says: Ask Me Another." Unlike the quiz shows of subsequent years, this was more of an educational program, where "Jack" would take questions from the announcer and answer them. There was no direct contact with the audience or with any other "expert." Still, the show was popular, and it led to an even more popular quiz show a few years later. This one was much more competitive: it featured teams from two rival Connecticut towns (Hartford and New Haven) in a battle of wits called "Quiz of Two Cities," sponsored by Listerine Toothpaste. The networks also got into quiz shows during the late 30s: "Information Please," "Professor Quiz," and "Kay Kyser's College of Musical Knowledge" were among the favorites.

Speaking of the networks, by 1934, another had come along (Mutual Broadcasting System), and CBS, which had never quite caught up with NBC, was making great strides in lining up important affiliates: by 1935, CBS was on 97 stations, and, more importantly, had won over former NBC affiliates such as WJR and KSL. This wasn't entirely because CBS had better programming; thanks to a clever arrangement that CBS' president William Paley designed, affiliates could carry as much or as little of CBS' offerings without cost (NBC charged affiliates $50 an hour for each unsponsored show they used), in exchange for CBS being allowed to carry some of the local affiliates' better shows on the network and selling the commercial time for them. The affiliates even shared the revenues from any shows for which CBS got sponsors. It was a good plan, especially during the Depression, when smaller stations had cash-flow worries and couldn't afford to pay much to a network.

As for the new Mutual Broadcasting network, despite the Depression, it made an immediate impact because of one program: " The Lone Ranger." First broadcast in 1933 over WXYZ in Detroit, the show, with its unique hero, struck a responsive chord, especially with children. During one show, popguns were offered to the first

400 kids who wrote in; in only 2 days, the station received nearly 25,000 letters. It wasn't long before WXYZ joined with WOR, WGN, and WLW to form "The Quality Group," which in late 1934, would become Mutual. These were the days of great creativity in radio, and Mutual brought forth some of the best, with series we still remember today. Thanks to Mutual, Americans were introduced to "Flash Gordon" in 1935 and to "The Green Hornet" in 1938. Mutual also debuted "The Adventures of Superman," "The Shadow," "The Cisco Kid," and "Hopalong Cassidy." Although other attempts to form networks failed, Mutual carved out a niche and did very well there.

If anyone still needed proof of radio's influence, CBS' broadcast of Sunday evening, October 30, 1938 made the point conclusively. That was the now-famous first broadcast of H.G. Wells' science-fiction classic, "The War of the Worlds," and although it was intended as a joke, millions of people took it seriously, convinced that Martians had indeed launched an invasion. Before we say that we are much more sophisticated today, note the continuing popularity of "professional wrestling" and how many fans believe that it's real. Radio, during its so-called golden age, had become so trusted, so believable, so much a part of the average person's life that the characters on the shows seemed like friends. Joseph Julian, a renowned radio actor of the 1930s and 40s, discussed this phenomenon in his memoirs, *This Was Radio*.

> (The broadcast itself) was actually a rather silly-looking spectacle: a group of unglamorous people sitting or strolling around a large room, holding sheets of paper in their hands, mumbling to themselves; going up to a microphone, delivering their lines, sitting down . . . A grown man jumps up and down in a sandbox to create the sound of running footsteps, or slaps his chest for horses' hoofbeats, or slowly crushes . . . cellophane to indicate a forest fire, while behind a glass panel, a man with a worried look on his face and a stop-watch in his hand makes 'stretch' or 'faster' signs for the performers . . . But, miraculously, all this nonsense came out the other end . . . in sounds that gripped, entertained and enthralled millions of Americans every day. Radio drama was the tranquilizer, the emotional pain-killing drug of the time. It made life more bearable for the isolated, the lonely, and the frustrated, who, by identifying with the characters, daily achieved some degree of catharsis. No other art form ever engaged the imagination more intensely (than radio).

Radio actors were definitely becoming stars, despite the critics who sneered at them and said they weren't as talented as theater actors. The public (and the sponsors) thought otherwise, however. Julian saw his salary grow from the $5 per show he made, along with hundreds of other out-of-work actors during the Depression, doing the crowd noises for "The March of Time" to $500 per show when he had lead roles. Radio drama had become an art, with its own sound-effects specialists and studio musicians who could deliver the right mood music on cue. Sponsors were especially pleased with radio dramas, because even the mention of a certain product by a character could bring about a rise in sales (as when on a soap opera, "Helen Trent" said she preferred a certain face cream, and thousands of women decided to try some).

Speaking of art forms, the commercial was becoming one too. Perhaps the first example of a singing jingle occurred on WCCO in the mid-20s. WCCO stood for Washburn Crosby Company, which would later become General Mills. The company was trying to market a new breakfast cereal, Wheaties, and results weren't very positive. Then the station hired a male quartet to extol the product, and a song about Wheaties was written. "The Wheaties Quartette" entertained Minneapolis through the 30s, and they put Wheaties on the map. Thanks to huge sales in the WCCO listening area, General Mills decided to have Wheaties sponsor baseball games on the station. This sports tie-in also did well, and led to Wheaties sponsoring baseball in 67 cities.

Radio had established itself as a comfort to the audience; it helped people cope in times of crisis. During the Depression especially, stations in the hardest-hit areas took this role to heart. WSB organized the first marathon charity program in 1932, raising $4000 to buy Christmas presents for the needy. KTSM, the only station in El Paso, provided listeners with the opportunity to express their opinions through person-in-the-street interviews, while entertaining them with a humorous morning show featuring "Karl the Kowhand," who told jokes, sang, and played the ukelele. ("Karl" was actually owner Karl Wyler, who did a little of everything in the station's early years.) KMA broadcast a number of fun events from local fairs: to us today, airing milking, pancake-eating, and egg-throwing contests might seem foolish, but the farmers really appreciated it. On a more serious note, KMA used its influence to give farmers a greater voice in government, keeping them informed about any pending legislation that might affect them, and offering them access to their elected officials.

Now that radio had become so pervasive in the society, its own local announcers were becoming very popular. More and more stations noticed that listeners paid close attention to what certain announcers said; sponsors also noticed this and put it to good use in testimonial commercials. People were attending station functions not only to meet whatever celebrity was there, but to shake hands with the announcers they heard every day. Some announcers were regarded as heroes, with as much fame on the local level as network stars enjoyed. In addition to listener adulation, they were also getting bigger paychecks in many cities, thanks to ever-increasing advertising revenues. Although not all announcers benefited financially, the role of the announcer was appreciated much more in the 30s, and the stage was set for some soon-to-be-legendary personalities to show their talents. One of them was Bob Steele of WTIC. Steele's main interest was sports, but when he joined the station in 1936, he was put to work reading commercials and doing station breaks. His voice was so well received that he soon built a following. As a sports reporter, he became known for his predictions (which were usually wrong), but his affable style led him to a career doing the morning show, which he was still doing in 1989!

Phonograph records were making a comeback, especially after 1929, when 33 1/3 electrical transcriptions (ETs) enabled announcers to play longer selections with better fidelity. Although KDKA and WJZ had pioneered using records, most stations in the 1920s and early 30s chose live performances. This was official policy at the networks: no recordings were allowed at all, except for sound effects. Thus, shows like "The March of Time" had to rely on skilled imitators to re-create the voices of the past week's newsmakers. The good side of the "live only" rule was that a lucrative industry sprung up, comprised of actors and actresses who could do animal noises, baby talk, or unusual foreign accents. The down side was that all network shows had to be performed twice: once for the East Coast, and then again, 3 hours later for the West Coast.

Another musical change in the early 30s was that large studio orchestras were slowly being phased out. Part of this was their cost, but the rest was due to the success of the Hammond organ at delivering mood music for network shows. Now that recorded music had improved, stations could also use records instead of live orchestras. This was a blessing in those cities where good musicians were scarce.

The transition from announcer (serious, pedantic, with an oratorical style) to disc jockey (warm, conversational, almost like a friend) was a gradual process. As for the very first DJ, KDKA's Frank Conrad played recorded music before anyone else did, but the idea didn't catch on; Harold Arlin of KDKA also played some records, as did Tommy Cowan of WJZ. Both Halloween Martin of KYW and Franklin Wintker of WLS in Chicago were "pancake turners"—the derisive name the musicians' union had for anyone who played records instead of using live performers. Until the mid-30s, these people were the exceptions. Speaking of exceptions, Norman Brokenshire, whose long and influential career began at WJZ in the early 20s, was regarded as the forerunner of personality announcers. Unlike most of his peers, he rebelled at reading prepared scripts or sounding professorial. His ad-libs and sly humor frustrated his bosses but delighted his listeners.

The changeover to recorded music made the record companies very happy. Back then, radio airplay was not expected to sell records; in fact, there often weren't records to sell because certain stars refused to make any. Other stars did make records but refused to allow radio to play them: Bing Crosby and Fred Waring were among those who even put warning labels on their records, stating that radio play was forbidden. Their reason was the fear that radio airplay would undermine their network contracts, in which they had promised the networks exclusive rights to their performances.

The FCC too seemed to be in favor of live music. Through the 1930s, any recorded music had to be repeatedly identified as such so that people would know they weren't hearing a live concert. The implication seemed to be that recorded music somehow wasn't as authentic as music performed live. Tensions ran high in some cities, as musicians protested what they saw as a dangerous trend. It was 1940 before the FCC eased the rule about how often stations were required to say that a song was recorded rather than live. It was also not until 1940 that the courts ruled that radio stations had the right to play an artist's records, whether the artist liked it or not; the warning notices on the record were not legally binding. These changes contributed even more to the rise of the DJ.

One by-product of the new acceptance of recorded music was the appearance of *hits*. Now that radio stations were able to play recorded music (the live musicians were still very upset about this, as they saw their jobs vanishing; by 1942, the president of the American Federation of Musicians noted sadly that over 500 radio stations no longer had studio orchestras or employed musicians), certain records received great approval from listeners, who wrote in their requests by the thousands. Add to that the rise in popularity of the jukebox, and the record companies suddenly found themselves with a gold mine.

Not every station fired all its live musicians: stations which had long-running or successful live shows tended to keep offering them, while adding the playing of phonograph records as just another new feature. Some stations like WTIC would continue to present live performances, including the Hartford Symphony, well into the 1950s.

At the same time though, WTIC saw the value of recorded music: Hartford was a major stop for most big bands and vocalists who were touring the East Coast, and fans who saw these people perform also wanted to hear their songs on radio. So WTIC obliged with Ross Miller, the station's first DJ. Miller didn't start until the late 40s, but he quickly made up for lost time—he was known for his rhymed introductions to the records he played; he called them "jukebox jingles," and called himself "Ross the Musical Boss." He also interviewed the stars and then played their latest song, a common practice today, but still new then.

The DJ show as we know it probably grew out of the work of Martin Block of WNEW in New York. Block admits he was heavily influenced by Al Jarvis of KFWB in Los Angeles. When Block worked in California, he heard Jarvis hosting a show called "The World's Largest Make-Believe Ballroom." (Not only was Jarvis one of the West Coast's most successful DJs, he also was a hit-maker who helped launch the career of big-band legend Benny Goodman.) When Block started at WNEW, he decided to try Jarvis's concept there. Martin Block's version went on the air as filler; it was 1935, mid-Depression, and WNEW had few expectations for a show where someone played records and tried to evoke a ballroom in the listener's mind. Block even had to buy his own records and get his own sponsor. To the management's surprise, the show built such an audience that by 1941, it was getting 12,000 fan letters a month, had 23 sponsors, and a waiting list of other interested advertisers.

It would be nice to say that the owners were won over to the disc jockeys' side by newfound respect for how talented these DJs were. At a few stations, that may have been true, but more often than not, what won the owners over was economics. Hiring a disc jockey cost a lot less than hiring an announcer and a studio orchestra ever did, and DJs often brought in their own sponsors, while merchandising their shows by appearances at stores.

Also, it was rather exciting to be responsible for a hit record. One example of this new pastime occurred in 1947, when Kurt Webster, "The Midnight Mayor" of WBT played a record he liked, a 1931 song by Ted Weems that had been out of print for years. The song began receiving so many requests that Weems' entire career was rejuvenated. His record company gave the young DJ an all-expense-paid week in New York to say "thank you"; Weems came to Charlotte to perform live, and he gave the proceeds of that concert to Webster.

As DJs became more influential, many of them also got rich: Al Jarvis signed a contract for $245,000 a year, during the 1940s. The owners saw the benefit in having high-profile DJs who enabled stations to increase listenership without putting too huge a dent in the bottom line. By the late 40s, even John Gambling, one of the original morning show hosts, no longer had his own studio orchestra; he too was playing records.

Although recorded music and personality announcers were becoming part of radio (and essential to what would become Full-Service), local news took on even more importance. Stations found that they could "scoop" the newspaper. Natural disasters, such as floods or hurricanes, made weather forecasting an especially valuable service, and stations began seeking out more complete information; some even hired meteorologists.

The gathering of news was helped greatly by the wire services: United Press International (UPI) was the first in 1935. [Although American stations were delighted, French-Canadian stations like CKAC were put at a disadvantage, since the news reports were all sent in English only. This meant CKAC had to lose valuable time translating stories. By 1938, however, wire service reports were available in French; this was augmented in 1941 by the Canadian Broadcasting Corporation (CBC) which set up a French language news bureau in Montreal.] Wire services gave local stations greater access to national stories.

As was happening with announcers, news reporters were also becoming well known and trusted. Local stations quickly saw that they could give a national news story a local twist and increase the audience's interest. During World War II, many stations held drives to sell war bonds, offering helpful cooking tips to the many housewives unable to obtain sugar or meat and keeping the local audience informed with the latest interviews from Red Cross workers or state representatives. As the need to be informed grew, stations hired stringers to contribute to their expanding news coverage. Some of these stringers would go on to become famous—CBS-TV anchor Walter Cronkite started as a stringer at WMT.

Investigative news was a while off, however. At the networks especially, and to some degree at the local level, the aim was to never rock the boat, to avoid offending sponsors (or potential sponsors). Joseph Julian wanted to do a program about racism in the U.S. army; CBS executives told him it was a "divisive issue" and refused to air it.

There was an unspoken ban on shows about societal problems during most of the 1930s, with the silence being broken by the occasional demagogue or would-be messiah who bought time to espouse a point of view. Networks tried their best to be seen as sources of entertainment; there was little room for controversy. (This stance was not restricted to radio; Hollywood had the same general attitude during the 30s. The movie-makers were limited by a rigid censorship system.) The local stations generally tried to stay away from negative stories; as late as 1935, WLW, which would go on to establish an excellent news department, issued memos telling news reporters they must never mention any strike or school walkout. An instructor trying to teach an on-air course in "modern problems" found that management censored his scripts. As respected a radio executive as CBS' William Paley went so far as to say that broadcasters should never make their personal views known or editorialize in any way. He stated in *Broadcasting Magazine* in December, 1937, "We must never try to further either side of any debatable question."

That neutrality was noble in theory, but as the 1930s came to a close and the question of United States involvement in World War II was on everyone's mind, commentary appeared almost everywhere, with radio providing a needed forum for the debate. Some of the most respected names in radio news came to the forefront as a result of covering the war, notably Edward R. Murrow and Howard K. Smith, to go along with the commentary of Lowell Thomas and H. V. Kaltenborn. (Kaltenborn had always believed in editorializing, much to the chagrin of the political figures he frequently criticized. As a result of this, he was frequently without a sponsor, which was the way he preferred it.)

News coverage continued to increase because the War was on the minds of so many people, but other than that, discussions of the social issues of the day were rare. Local stations had moved away from the earlier belief that only *events* (presidential elections, the Lindbergh baby-kidnapping trial) were newsworthy. Now, day-to-day coverage of local occurrences was much more common, even if those occurrences weren't as dramatic as a flood or a hurricane.

However, radio was a mainly white medium. It is no accident that two white men (in blackface) played the roles of "Amos 'n' Andy." There were a few black musicians, but in general, radio in the 30s and 40s made no effort to hire minorities. Black actors were offered occasional parts, but only as servants or menials; ironically, these black actors (and actresses) were instructed to talk in an exaggerated dialect so that they would "sound more like a Negro." Even those radio owners in predominantly black cities shied away from discussing racial problems on the air and would not hire black announcers.

In 1935, there were only two black announcers—one was Jack Cooper, of WSBC in Chicago, believed to be the very first. Cooper went on to an illustrious career, during which he was also a newscaster and later a station executive. His first show was called the "All-Colored Hour," a variety show which featured black music, perhaps the pioneering effort in this genre.

However, Cooper and Jocko Maxwell, the other black announcer (he did sports for WHOM, Jersey City), were fighting against deeply ingrained attitudes (the same attitudes that kept women off the air by and large until the 1970s). In fact, as late as 1947, there were only 16 black DJs, according to *Ebony Magazine*. The first black-owned station wouldn't appear till 1949, 1 year after WDIA in Memphis became the first station to play black music, using black announcers.

Until that year, the experience of Vernon Winslow was the norm in most cities. Winslow was an educator and a journalist; he wrote a column for a black newspaper in New Orleans, using the pen name "Poppa Stoppa." The column, which addressed issues of concern to blacks, was written in a popular rhyming slang called *jive*. Encouraged by the success of his column, Winslow decided that Poppa Stoppa would do well on radio; New Orleans had a large black population, and surely it made good business sense to give them some entertainment of their own. It was the late 30s, however, and Winslow's idea was considered too radical. Finally, WMJR radio agreed to hire Poppa Stoppa, but under one condition: Winslow would write the scripts and then train a white announcer to read them. So it was that Vernon Winslow spent his days teaching white announcers to talk jive, never allowed to portray the character he had created. Poppa Stoppa did become a hit in New Orleans. Winslow eventually went on to host a successful rhythm-and-blues variety show at another station.

If this all seems like a history lesson, the reason for mentioning it is that no radio format has ever been created in a vacuum. There were many factors which contributed to the development of Full-Service, and societal conditions did play a part. True, it was a time of many taboos: not only were racism and sexism seldom discussed, but neither were divorce, child abuse or alcoholism. Radio had evolved at a time when certain tabloid newspapers became famous for dwelling on crime and scandal. Many owners wanted radio to be a safe, family-oriented medium, and as such, they were reticent to discuss subjects that might shock the listeners.

As World War II broke out, however, the networks reacted to what they saw as patriotic fervor, by airing some rather one-sided diatribes that were supposedly news but in reality were anti-Japanese or anti-German tirades. These "know your enemy" broadcasts evoked the same hysteria that Father Coughlin did. This was especially ironic given that the National Association of Broadcasters had issued a strong statement against biased news programs in the new code they adopted in 1939. The War Department and the Office of War Information wanted to present a united, pro-American point of view on radio, and their influence, while perhaps done with good intentions, led to an implicit censorship of any views considered "subversive."

Even in wartime though, some courageous stations refused to go along with what they saw as a disturbing trend. WTIC, mindful of its promise to serve "in the public interest," established a policy that they would refuse to air propaganda, no matter which nationality was the subject. WTIC's management had always been proud of the station's good name and its reputation for objectivity and accuracy. There was no room for hate-mongering under any circumstances.

It would be unfair to say that all stations of the late 30s ignored social problems or avoided controversy. Some stations developed a strong community image that has lasted to this day. WGN in Chicago became known for its educational programs, featuring distinguished educators; the station even offered on-air courses, one of which was about current economic and social issues that affected Chicagoans. WBZ in Boston, the first station to broadcast the Boston Symphony Orchestra and the Boston Pops, could also take charge during a crisis: in 1936, during a major flood in western Massachusetts, WBZ announcers and engineers flew to Springfield and donated both time and equipment, helping flood victims and rescue workers. WTIC was the voice of sanity during a 1938 hurricane, offering reliable information instead of rumors.

A few stations even confronted the race issue. WCCO, which, ironically, didn't have a full-time news department till 1943, aired a documentary about racial discrimination called "Neither Free Nor Equal." WSB produced an award-winning series that discussed prejudice and the problems of youth; it was called "The Harbor We Seek." Even CBS, which had not been willing to talk about segregation in the army, presented an eloquent commentary, "An Open Letter on Race Hatred" as a response to the Detroit race riots of 1943 that left hundreds injured and 34 dead. The program earned much critical praise, but many CBS affiliates in the South refused to carry it.

Still, it was encouraging that CBS offered a show on a theme long regarded as unmentionable.

In the mid-40s, as radio's golden age was about to end, Paul Harvey had just joined WENR in Chicago. "The Adventures of Ozzie and Harriet" first appeared in that same year, 1944. Mike Wallace, who would later become the co-host of TV's popular "60 Minutes," had just gotten out of the navy. Abbott and Costello were doing well in radio, after being successful in both vaudeville and movies. Alan Freed, considered by many to be the founding father of rock and roll radio DJs, was turned down by CBS in New York and was working at WAKR in Akron as a newscaster. Quiz shows were still popular, as were radio dramas. There was a new network (ABC). Sportscaster Curt Gowdy had moved up from KBFC in Cheyenne, Wyoming, to KOMA in Oklahoma City. Ed Sullivan, whose TV variety show would ultimately feature Elvis Presley and the Beatles, was beginning his radio career, as was singer Perry Como. There were about 40 FMs on the air, but few people noticed since all the popular programs were on AM. New AMs were appearing in small markets. Television was off to a slow start. The concept of *format* was beginning to emerge. Soon, this concept would become much more clearly defined and change radio broadcasting dramatically.

4

Full-Service as a Format

By the time the war was ending, a number of stations had already established a tradition of community service. News coverage had expanded because of the war, but for these stations, there was also an obligation to keep the audience informed in other ways. To demonstrate pride in their state, the staff of WSB produced a series of half-hour salutes, and they traveled all over Georgia paying tribute to all 159 of its counties. As WTIC had done during hurricanes, WSB brought reassurance and calm to Atlanta when a tragic hotel fire killed 119 people in late 1946; the station suspended regular broadcasting and served as an information conduit, airing appeals for extra medical personnel and blood donations, as well as giving the list of survivors and helping them find shelter. KMA, which had begun church services for shut-ins and inspired hundreds of donations of wheelchairs, blankets, and even radios for invalids during the 1930s, continued into the 40s with other humanitarian efforts, including the Iowa Rural School Graduation Program. This unique event allowed students from small, rural schools that lacked resources for graduation ceremonies to be honored at the KMA auditorium. KDKA, one of the very first stations to do community service, was even more actively involved than ever, creating a campaign with Pittsburgh's Children's Hospital resulting in free medical care for hundreds of needy local kids. Many stations had "Town Meeting of the Air" programs to discuss local issues; WBZ even introduced a "Junior Town Meeting" so that students could express their views. The fears that some early critics of commercial radio had express-ed proved to be unfounded, for these stations, while still making a profit, had not forgotten that their primary responsibility was to serve their market in a positive manner.

In addition to a tradition of service, stations had also begun a tradition of successful locally produced entertainment programs, some of which went on to national fame. Among the earliest (1925) was "Grand Old Opry," which originated in Nashville at WSM ("*We Shield Millions*"—the station was owned by the National Life and Accident Insurance Company). The show was first called the "WSM Barn Dance," and it aired from a tiny studio. Years later, the show is still going strong, has a large TV audience, and has launched the careers of hundreds of country stars. Another music show with great longevity is a bit more serious: KSL in Salt Lake City began broadcasting live performances by the Mormon Tabernacle Choir in 1929. Then, there's the amazing story of "The Little Red Barn," a good-time country music show that went on the air at WOWO, Fort Wayne, in 1945. Hosted by local performers Sam DeVincent and his wife Nancy Lee, the show stayed in its early Sunday morning time slot through numerous station format changes and even new owners. Sam and Nancy received the ultimate accolade in late 1989, when CBS Radio Network correspondent Charles Osgood paid tribute to their popular show on an edition of "The Osgood File." In addition to these long-running local shows, the networks had some entertainment shows too: In the late 1940s, Bob Hope, Jack Benny, and Bing Crosby were well into their second decade of radio stardom. Some of the early 30s soap operas were still around, most notably "Ma Perkins" and "The Romance of Helen Trent." In fact, radio seemed to have it all: established national programs, local shows with sizeable audiences, and a number of profitable stations which had also built solid reputations for news and community service. Then suddenly, everything changed again, thanks in large part to the rise of television.

The new technologies perfected in the late 40s and early 50s both helped and hurt radio. On the plus side, there were improvements in car radios, such that by 1946, nine million automobiles had them. Also, in 1946, came the introduction of the clock radio. First developed by General Electric, it sold well and people liked its features, especially the snooze alarm. News departments were delighted when, in 1947, there were big improvements in tape recorders. The small, portable transistor radio finally went on sale in 1953, after some experiments in 1948. Now radio could truly go anywhere.

On the other hand, there was TV. It would be facile to say that video killed the radio star, but it certainly complicated matters. TV was really not a new invention—Vladimir Zworykin had done some experiments as early as 1917. He came to the United States in 1919, and ultimately went to work for David Sarnoff at RCA, continuing his research well into the 30s. Another early pioneer of TV was Philo Farnsworth, who was able to transmit a picture by 1927. He worked for Philadelphia Storage Battery Company (Philco) for a while, but eventually got some backers and continued his experiments on his own. In both England and Canada, similar experiments with TV were ongoing during the early 30s, and it seemed a matter of time before a major breakthrough occurred.

In reality, television sets weren't ready for sale in the United States until 1938 (1936 in England). There were only four brands at first, ranging in price from $125 up to $600. However, the FCC didn't think TV was quite ready, even referring to it as experimentation that might prove to have no usefulness! Not until 1940 were a few stations permitted to have limited commercial operation. The war slowed the drive to expand TV; as World War II ended, there were still only six TV stations, and they operated only a few hours a day, much as radio had when it was still new.

By 1948, growth was still slow. The public wasn't yet sure about this new medium, constructing a TV station could be very expensive, and the equipment was still very complicated. There were only 34 stations by this time, a few owned by large AM stations whose owners used some radio profits to get in on the ground floor of what they foresaw as the next big trend. WSB in Atlanta and WBT in Charlotte were among the successful AM stations which entered into TV. The radio networks became involved too, especially NBC, which had the resources necessary to shoulder the expense of TV stations. NBC had an informal 4-station TV network by 1946, and within the next 2 years, it increased to 25. The other networks got involved as well, to the degree their finances permitted, and within 6 years, coast-to-coast TV networks were a reality.

Meanwhile, as with radio in its infancy, complications had beset TV. The FCC was receiving more applications for TV stations. New York needed 7 channels, out of the 13 that had been allocated. The original plan was to have stations in different cities, at least 200 miles apart, sharing channels, but this wouldn't work for the many good-sized cities that were within 200 miles of New York and wanted TV. As a compromise, it was decided that East Coast stations would only be 150 miles apart, but unfortunately, this resulted in severe interference problems. Complaints mounted and led to the FCC putting a total freeze on all new TV licenses as of September 1948. It was only supposed to be temporary, to allow the FCC to devise a workable solution, as well as to make some room somewhere on the television band for an educational channel. There were also controversies over color TV, setting new technical standards, and the future possibility of more than 13 channels. Of course, the stations already on the air were in no hurry to see the freeze lifted and new competition allowed. With all the committees needed to study the situation, considerable infighting resulted, and in the end, the "temporary" freeze wasn't lifted until 1952.

Radio during the freeze was still prosperous: many cities didn't yet have TV, and who could predict when they would? Radio dramas remained popular, as did quiz shows. One highly rated program required a knowledge of music and listener loyalty. "Stop the Music" began on ABC in 1948, and the rules were simple: the studio orchestra played a song, while host Bert Parks made a random phone call. The person who could name the song just played won a big prize. Another music-oriented show wasn't a quiz, but did have suspense. "Your Hit Parade" had been introduced on network radio in 1935 and was still doing fine in the late 40s. Here, eager fans could hear the latest hits by Perry Como or Nat "King" Cole. Having a song chosen to be performed on the show was considered a big honor and assured the song's success. Nobody seemed to know what criteria were used to define a hit, but each Saturday night, listeners waited patiently to find out which songs had made the show's Top-10. It was not TV that ended "Your Hit Parade" (the show moved to TV in 1950). Rather, the rise of Top-40 music caused its demise. As rock and roll, music the cast clearly didn't like or feel comfortable singing, became popular, fans didn't want to hear a member of "Your Hit Parade" perform the hits—they wanted to hear the same version they were hearing over and over on Top-40 radio. The show couldn't adapt.

Radio in the late 40s still boasted many famous comedians and the best-known big bands. Frank Sinatra, beloved by legions of female fans, often performed, as did other leading vocalists of the era. There was also gossip-columnist supreme Walter Winchell, still intermingling news stories with the latest celebrity scandals. There were detective shows, mysteries, and westerns. On the local level, announcers like Grady Cole of WBT were in the midst of long and illustrious careers. (Cole would remain the station's morning show host for 30 years; despite a gravelly voice, his wry humor and folksy style made him an idol in Charlotte.) Advertisers still believed in radio.

When the freeze on new TV stations ended, the United States was in the midst of a very controversial and frightening period of time: the McCarthy era. There was no "glasnost" in those days; Russia was regarded as an enemy, and to be called a "communist" was an insult. Senator Joseph McCarthy believed there were communist sympathizers in positions of power in the United States, and he was determined to find them. Beginning in the summer of 1950 with the publication of *Red Channels: The Report of Communist Influence in Radio and TV*, McCarthy embarked upon a witch-hunt of epic proportions. The book was filled with inaccuracies and unproven allegations, yet hundreds of innocent people lost their jobs as a result; worse, they lost their good name and were given no opportunity to clear it. Blacklisting became common—if your name were in the book, no matter how much you protested, suddenly no one would hire you. Joe Julian, one of the busiest and most in-demand radio actors of the 1930s and 40s, saw his income dwindle to almost nothing, and even people he thought were his friends wouldn't return his calls. All this happened because the man who compiled the book, Vincent Hartnett, decided that a group Julian had belonged to in 1942 was really a subversive communistic front. No proof was given, nor did Hartnett (or McCarthy) ever explain how they decided which groups were subversive and which ones weren't.

Meanwhile, McCarthy, who knew how to stir a radio audience to a fever pitch with talk about traitors and spies, went about his task virtually unchallenged, ruining many lives along the way. Like Father Coughlin before him, McCarthy had touched a nerve; fear and suspicion ruled.

Interestingly, it was television that proved Joseph McCarthy's undoing, thanks to the courageous efforts of news reporter Edward R. Murrow. Murrow now had a TV show, "See It Now," and after ignoring McCarthy for a long while, finally agreed to show him for who he really was. On radio, the senator sounded rather imposing; on TV, he just looked like a demagogue. It was the first of many times when presidential candidates or political figures would rise or fall as a result of how they presented themselves on TV. McCarthy resembled a petty, vindictive tyrant, and as people had the opportunity to observe him more closely, they didn't like what they saw, making it easier for saner voices to question him. Gradually, his reign of terror ended.

Cutting McCarthy down to size may have been the only favor TV did for radio in the early 50s. Now that there were more stations, reception had improved, and TV sets were readily available, many radio stars jumped to the new medium. (For most it worked well, but as with McCarthy, some radio performers just didn't translate well to TV, even though they tried.)

As network radio stars moved on, so did some of radio's better dramas, which soon were changed into TV shows. Morale at the radio networks was low: it seemed all the big names were giving up on radio. Television seemed to have the momentum.

Further, TV had won friends in the advertising community. Initially skeptical, now sponsors saw that TV got them results: one cosmetic company had been doing about a $50,000 annual business when it first bought some TV commercials in 1950, and by 1952 that same company had an income of $4.5 million. Network advertising on TV grew from $2.5 to $172 million in 1953. Meanwhile, radio advertising had declined, although in 1952, radio still did $103 million in national business. The problem was that since the end of the war, more radio stations had gone on the air, bringing the total of AMs in 1953 to 2391; this sliced the national dollars even thinner. Some radio owners pondered their future, wondering if they still had one. Then, with another parallel to radio's early days, suddenly, the novelty of TV wore off.

Once it wasn't new and exciting, TV simply took its place in people's lives; viewers even became more selective about what they wanted to watch. As matters stabilized, another fact became evident: there was still room for radio. People who commuted to work in increasing numbers put their car radios to good use. The clock radio was an item few people lacked; it was a much more humane way of waking up than by just a noisy alarm clock.

Radio stations themselves were refusing to give up; from the 50,000-watt stations like KMOX in St. Louis and WBAL in Baltimore, to the lower-powered stations in the smallest towns, stations worked hard to remain useful to the audience. For some, that meant expanding local news. For others, it meant taking a few chances, such as putting on talk shows about controversial subjects. (Again, by contemporary standards, these shows were quite tame, but in a very conservative era, discussing venereal disease or teenage pregnancy on radio was very unusual.) Others just kept doing what they did best: KMOX and WBAL had major-league sports and excellent signals. WOWO and WBT kept giving local musicians valuable radio exposure. WMT established a midday interview show, "The Voice of Iowa," which solicited listener opinion at a variety of local events and was a part of the station for 30 years. KMA and WHO expanded their farm news. WCCO added more personality announcers. WTIC created the "Travelers Weather Service" and developed forecasting procedures that would enable listeners to know what the weather would probably be several days ahead. WSB became involved in promotions to increase awareness of radio; one station executive even stated that he was glad TV had come along to shake radio out of its lethargy and force it to become more exciting.

The controversial move of WDIA in Memphis to Black radio in the late 40s became an idea whose time had come in the 50s. Looking for new ways to attract the evening audience when people were supposedly all watching TV, some radio stations began playing *race music*, or rhythm and blues. This music seemed to attract young blacks, but whites liked it too, and it was the forerunner of rock and roll.

The old guard of radio was gone, but that opened the door for some new thinking and some new personality DJs. By the 1950s, the majority of the stations that played music did so in an almost predictable context: news on the hour, music, commercials, weather, time checks, and some announcer chatter. Some stations weren't playing the music they once played: WSB and WBT were moving away from Country to a more pop sound, as was WOWO. Few stations played any Big Band or orchestra music anymore; WTIC was among the last holdouts, in fact. Classical music was now on FM, along with some other "serious" music, but FM still wasn't hurting AM's listener base.

It was time for the event that changed radio even more than TV did: the emergence of Top-40. How exactly this format was invented is still a source of debate;

some say it started in New Orleans in 1953. Others say it began in Omaha in 1955. The idea of playing hits, based on requests, could even be traced back to the 1940s or to "Make-Believe Ballroom." In any case, the sequence of events wasn't what made the impact: rock and roll did that, and in a major fashion.

The postwar baby-boom kids were in their early teens, and they couldn't relate to their parents' music. As the story goes, radio executive Todd Storz was sitting in an Omaha bar one night, talking with his assistant and people-watching. He observed a waitress playing the same song in the jukebox over and over, and from that, he deduced that people like to hear their favorite songs a lot. The rest is history. Storz put his theory into practice on KOWH, in 1955, with a reduced playlist and a "pick hit" of the week; the #1 song was played once every hour.

Meanwhile, the other person generally credited with founding the Top-40 format, Gordon McLendon, was in Dallas at KLIF, applying some of his own ideas. It was McLendon who introduced unique and outrageous promotions which made people remember the station, such as having an announcer broadcast from a glass booth in a parking lot or having a "mystery millionaire" stand on a street corner giving out money; McLendon also introduced the use of jingles (singing identifiers with the station's call letters). Storz was also a big believer in cash giveaways, and did many of them with great success.

Top-40 caught on quickly. The print media couldn't say enough bad things about the music; preachers accused rock and roll of leading young people into sin. The more adults berated it, however, the more young people loved it and the stations that played it. The good news for radio was that Top-40 brought an entirely new generation into the fold of radio listeners, a young generation that might grow along with the medium, guaranteeing it an audience for years to come.

The bad news was that these teenagers didn't want to hear Sinatra nor did they want anything that seemed old or boring to them. The traditional way radio had been done up till this point was very broad, with a wide spectrum of features, information, and popular 40s-style music. Suddenly, there was radio for teens and radio for everybody else. In some markets, the conservative and established stations just waited for this Top-40 fad to die out, but it only became more entrenched.

In Minneapolis, WCCO had a problem it had never had before: How could it combat the inroads Top-40 was making without compromising the image it had strived for with adults all these years? The problem was all the more acute because Todd Storz was in town, doing Top-40 at WDGY. So it was that WCCO did something it had not done in its entire 32 years: It decided to match Storz and give away money too. Using a cash register for sound effects, DJ Big Bill Cash got his first winner in March of 1956—the listener who knew the right phrase won $300.

Storz loved a good battle, even with a station that wasn't Top-40. WCCO gave away $30,000 in 6 months, which certainly generated excitement, but across town, Storz announced a new jackpot totaling $105,000. Not to be outdone when they'd come this far, the staff of WCCO then announced that they had a new jackpot too—$250,000, and on it went. Eventually, the silliness came to a merciful end, but WCCO derived a positive result for its investment: over half a million listeners had written to the station requesting to be entered in a prize drawing called "Cash Club."

Looking back on it later, the staff had to admit that, as expensive as the promotion had been, it energized the entire station. It also showed advertisers that while WCCO might be synonymous with public service and older music, that didn't mean the station had to be stodgy; it was willing to take on a competitor and have fun doing it. Incidents like this were not unique.

As the Top-40 format kept gaining, and as the teen audience became more viable to advertisers, stations had to evaluate how they wanted to address the fastest growing segment of the American population. In most cases, the KDKAs and the WTICs knew they wouldn't be able to attract teens on a regular basis, but these stations still found ways to reach out to the teen audience. Some stations, using their tradition of block programming, started a Saturday countdown show, which allowed them to play some teen music without overly upsetting the station's adult core listeners. Other stations began doing salutes to certain high school scholars or athletes. (A few stations decided that if you couldn't beat 'em, you might as well join 'em. WLS in Chicago, which had played Country in the early days and had done considerable farm service, became a Top-40 station in 1960, with great success.) Top-40 also did wonders for the record industry; now, the configuration of choice was the 45 rpm (the single), which jukebox companies also liked because their machines could hold more 45s than the 78s of earlier years.

The gradual but steady influence of teenagers and Top-40 would also lead to another change. Where the stations of the Golden Age of Radio tried to please everyone, offering the widest possible variety, the Top-40 stations aimed at only one narrow age group and didn't pretend to do otherwise. Agencies expected this narrowcasting approach to fail, but as more Top-40 stations rose to number one, and, surprisingly, attracted more than just teens, sponsors had to take a second look. Many successful adult radio stations did this too. Although not going as far as WLS and changing over to Top-40, these stations could see dramatic evidence that listening habits were changing, and they knew they had to adapt to the times.

One good example of this process was WBZ in Boston, long a source of cultural and political events. (In the early 1950s, WBZ frequently aired important addresses by the mayor, civic leaders, senators, and the governor.) WBZ greeted the 60s by becoming an interesting hybrid—playing some of the modern songs (without anything too loud) while keeping a stable and well-respected air staff and a strong news commitment. WBZ's announcers were definitely personalities; they did a lot more than just spin records. Similarly, WBZ was known for its reliable weather reports and a tradition of community service. So when the Doris Day and Perry Como songs vanished, some of the older listeners were upset, but most of WBZ's audience accepted the younger music and didn't miss all the political addresses. WBZ basically fine-tuned its programming to make it more applicable to the needs of their current audience, rather than simply remaining fixed in the way radio was done in the 40s. This compromise (a solid news commitment—WBZ ran 29 daily newscasts, including one full 30-minute report; news specials and documentaries; and the most listenable of the new pop hits) saved a number of stations, WBZ among them. The station was still informative, pleasant, and friendly—but now it sounded more contemporary.

Thus, a new format type emerged: It would eventually be called *Middle of the Road*, since it practiced a moderate approach to programming, with just the right amount of news and features, music that wasn't offensive, and personalities who understood the issues that concerned the average person. Some radio critics would also note that it was called Middle of the Road (soon abbreviated to MOR) because it was targeted at the middle class.

Although it didn't happen immediately, the late 1950s and early 60s saw much more emphasis on programming to a specific audience. Black stations were appearing in markets that had previously resisted them; these stations proved very influential, both in helping records become hits and in giving the black community a voice. Although the biggest and best MOR stations had not overtly ignored black charities, the truth was that most stations wanted to be as mass-appeal as possible, and ethnic programs were usually relegated to Sunday morning; the particular ethnic group usually had to pay the station for the time.

Thus, Black stations were able to carve out a niche that allowed them to specifically become involved in causes that were of particular concern to blacks, such as fighting sickle-cell anemia. As was happening with Top-40 versus MOR, Black stations too began to choose a certain demographic to serve, such as teens or 25- to 44-year-olds. Narrowcasting was slowly becoming a fact of life in radio programming. The days when stations chose their music or their presentation based on guesswork had long since ended—there had, as you know, been ratings available since 1930, and now, as radio became even more competitive and splintered into different age groups, renewed interest in ratings occurred.

Stations wanted to know how they were doing, not only to get their fair share of advertising dollars but to assure their position in their market. After Archibald Crossley and C.E. Hooper, the next company to do audience measurement was called "The Pulse Inc.," and unlike its predecessors, Pulse used home interviews instead of telephone recall. Crossley's company had folded in 1946, so it was either Hooper or Pulse if you wanted ratings in the 50s and early 60s. The competition between the two companies was intense: in 1958, Pulse was surveying about 200 markets and Hooper approximately 175.

Each claimed to be more reliable than the other; the truth was that both had drawbacks. Hooper's reliance on telephone surveying counted out anyone too poor to have a phone; since they derived their numbers from phone books, anyone with an unlisted phone number was also never counted. Pulse couldn't always find enough people willing to sit for a long, in-depth interview; critics of their methodology suggested that people who just wanted to get the interview over with might give inaccurate information. Neither service did an effective job with minorities either; homes in supposedly bad neighborhoods were often ignored, and people who spoke Spanish were at a disadvantage talking to interviewers who only spoke English. This became an issue in markets with large ethnic populations, such as Los Angeles. However, most agencies felt that some ratings were better than none, and despite the flaws, agencies looked first at a station's ratings before placing an advertising buy.

There was one other ratings service, American Research Bureau (ARB), but although it had been around since 1949, it hadn't made any inroads on Hooper or

Pulse. This changed, however, when ARB perfected a more efficient way of gathering ratings: sending listeners diaries to fill out and mail back. The beauty of this method was that it required neither phone calls nor personal interviews. Throughout the late 60s, ARB and its diary method gradually gained respect. By 1970, it was the dominant ratings service. (ARB changed its name to Arbitron in 1973. Hooper merged with another company, and Pulse eventually abandoned the ratings business entirely.) Arbitron too would be accused of not measuring blacks and Hispanics accurately and would see several other ratings services emerge in the 70s and 80s, most notably Birch.

As the demand for ratings information grew, they spread into even the smaller markets where ratings had previously been considered by some owners as an unnecessary expense. Now even these stations couldn't avoid being asked by sponsors to show their Arbitron results. Stations whose entire history had been based on serving their community were also being asked to document how effectively they reached their target audience. Almost by default, the target audience for MOR stations had become adults 35 years old and over.

New formats kept appearing throughout the 60s to further splinter the young audience. The most popular of these was Album Rock (which was at first called *progressive* or *free-form*), a format aimed at 18- to 24-year-old males. It also became popular on college campuses. Young adults who felt Top-40 was too repetitive and juvenile gravitated to Album Rock because it offered a hip image plus album tracks from the best rock groups, rather than just hit singles. Album Rock (later renamed AOR, *A*lbum *O*riented *R*ock by Mike Harrison, who during the mid-70s was an editor of the important music industry newspaper *Radio & Records*) became a viable FM format at a time when the FM band was still considered alternative and a good place to experiment.

Although MOR wasn't affected by AOR per se, it certainly found itself with a clear position: If Top-40 and AOR were for kids, then MOR, with its blend of news, information, and music, was perfect for grown-ups. Soon however, there were other successful adult formats too (such as Beautiful Music), and suddenly, the audience had many choices rather than just one or two.

MOR now found itself at a crossroad. With radio listeners becoming more selective, with new formats emerging to further fragment adult listening habits, with FM becoming more popular, could MOR compete? It had shown in the past that it was able to adapt, but could it do so now and could it still win? This was the challenge, and MOR prepared to meet it.

5
Full-Service Meets the Challenge

In 1952, Canada had finally gotten its first TV station, CBFT in Montreal, while in the United States, the freeze was over and new TV stations were springing up everywhere. With its biggest stars going over to TV and its best network shows ending, radio's future looked so bleak that even some of its own executives (David Sarnoff's son Robert among them) predicted that radio would soon be dead. Fortunately, reports of radio's death were somewhat premature.

Although the next several decades brought many changes, radio was very much alive and well as the 1970s began. It had survived the payola scandal of 1960 (much as TV would survive a similar quiz show scandal, during which it was revealed that the biggest winners had been given the answers and prepared in advance on at least three popular quiz shows). The payola hearings resulted in legislation which took music selection away from the announcers and put it in the hands of the program director; accepting any sort of bribe in exchange for radio airplay was now illegal. The critics of rock radio (it was rock DJs who were accused of accepting payola from record promoters) expected that the payola scandal would do great damage to Top-40's image, but Top-40 continued to be successful, even with new rules and tighter controls over music policy.

For the most part, MOR stations weren't touched by the payola scandal: most MOR stations didn't play the hits, and even when they did, it was usually after the song had been around for a while. Further, it was believed back then that people over 25 years old didn't buy records or go to concerts, so few record promoters courted MOR stations with the intensity applied to Top-40, where playing a new song first was very important. This left MOR to set up its own music policies, using research or just playing whatever might be comfortable and familiar to an older listener. The payola scandal came and went, but the question of what music to play at an MOR station remained an enigma. Listeners' tastes were becoming even more polarized.

The generation born in the late 40s and early 50s, the so-called "baby boomers," were entirely different from their parents. Part of this may have been youthful rebellion, but some of it was a reflection of the changes happening in the society at large: the Vietnam War, the civil rights movement, the introduction of recreational drugs into the middle class, etc. Baby boomers went to college, but many felt no obligation to stay. They wore clothes their parents considered outrageous. They liked music that was often loud with unintelligible lyrics, yet they also appreciated the complex imagery of such singer-songwriters as Bob Dylan and Paul Simon. Many used drugs and remained oblivious to current events, but just as many marched for equality or protested the war.

Meanwhile, more women were entering the work force, some in nontraditional jobs. FM radio was becoming increasingly popular. AM Top-40 stations were being challenged by tightly formatted Album Rock on FM, and advertising revenues on FM were continuing to climb. By the mid-70s, FM rock stations were winning the young adult ratings wars in many cities. Even Country radio found its audience fragmenting into two groups: those who preferred the old, traditional Country and Western music and those who wanted the more contemporary sounds of modern Country artists.

Formats seemed to be getting more and more narrow, attention spans shorter, people in more of a hurry. Studies from academia lamented that young people didn't read as much as they used to, and a number of magazines went out of business. As the young adults raised with Top-40's frenetic pace got older, they brought with them their tendency to button-push, that is, they had no exclusive loyalty to any one station and would dial around until they heard something they liked.

All of these factors contributed to the confusion MOR programmers felt. They had inherited a devoted audience that came to MOR for sports, news, public service information, and the music that brought back the good memories. These listeners were in large part over 40 years old. They didn't like screaming DJs and they had no use for Elvis Presley. They liked songs with words they could sing along with, and they didn't like suggestive lyrics. They expected the announcers to be knowledgeable and friendly.

Advertisers, however, were very actively pursuing the youth market, and as the baby boomers gradually aged, the 25- to 34-year-old demographic became the most eagerly sought: that group was supposed to have money to spend, and unlike their parents (who had put theirs in savings accounts), those people wanted certain things and weren't willing to save for 20 years to get them. Buying on credit became common, and the use of credit cards flourished.

MOR stations had always been able to deliver a loyal audience for the advertiser's message, but as ratings information showed, MOR listeners were seldom aged 25 to 34. Not wanting to lose all those advertising dollars, especially when FMs were providing even more competition, MOR stations pondered their direction. Some, as mentioned earlier, found that the way WBZ adapted made sense for them too, but such modification wasn't always easy. Some older listeners protested vehemently when the music of the 1940s was replaced by soft rock, but more than the older audience, some of the older announcers weren't pleased when they learned their companies intended to appeal to a slightly younger demographic.

Ed Salamon, who went on to become president of programming for the Unistar Radio Network, was the music director of KDKA in the early 70s. He recalls that some of the announcers were so upset that they would bring older music from their own personal collections into the station secretly, and play these songs when they thought he wasn't around. Like WBZ, though, KDKA too found that a blend of pleasant modern music along with the services for which they had became so well known meant that 25- to 34-year-olds who sampled the station found it appealing. True, most baby boomers had grown up listening to Top-40, a format that didn't stress news or information (although Top-40 stations did have small doses of both elements); the theory was that as the boomers grew up, married, and had kids of their own, they would welcome a station that gave them not just the hits but lots of useful and interesting information as well.

Unfortunately for MOR, with the rise of FM also evolved a new permutation of adult-oriented programming. Ironically, given the original reasons for MOR, this new version attempted to be the next middle of the road, only this time, the two extremes were Top-40 (too frantic for adults) and traditional MOR itself (too much talk, not enough music).

The new format became known as *Adult Contemporary* (or AC) because it was aimed at adults yet had a modern image. AC stations played the popular hits by current and recent artists, as well as some *oldies,* or hits from when the baby boomers were teenagers. Like some of the MORs, AC music was never loud or strident. It was familiar, comfortable, and hit-oriented (unlike *Beautiful Music*, a format popular with older adults on FM—Beautifuls would play alternative versions of a hit song or lush instrumental versions, whereas AC would only play the version that had been the original hit). AC stations offered news and information, but music was a major part of what they did, while by now, the majority of MOR stations had become successful as a result of their nonmusic elements. While AC stations (also called *Lite Rock* or *Soft Rock*) became popular (especially with females, on the FM band, capturing sizeable numbers in that 25- to 34-year-old age group), MORs mostly remained on the AM band.

As with WCCO when the station had tried to compete head on with a Top-40, most MORs quickly realized that they couldn't pretend to be AC any more than they could have pretended to be Top-40. So for the astute managers at MOR stations, this meant exploring new ways of serving the audience while still maintaining the commitment of Full-Service radio.

The fragmentation still wasn't done. By the early 1980s, there were other new formats, as well as changes in several of the older ones. Even Top-40 (so called because in its original form, it had only played 40 records, over and over) wasn't Top-40 anymore; it was renamed *Contemporary Hit Radio* (CHR). This occurred as a result of the intense competition for that 25- to 34-year-old audience. Since pure Top-40 was allegedly popular mainly with teens, certain key Top-40 stations tried to slightly soften their sound in the hope that more adults would listen if there were fewer teen-oriented (hard rock) songs on their playlist. Soon, some Top-40s were sounding almost Adult Contemporary, hence the new name.

Oldies stations also became increasingly more popular, on both AMs and FMs. A new phenomenon was now taking place as the population gradually aged. Where years ago, only teens bought records and few people past college age attended rock concerts, these were the new members of the 25- to 34- and 35- to 44-year-old age groups. They came to this time in their lives still loving rock music. Though perhaps they didn't care for the extremes any more (heavy metal or punk rock, for example), they weren't ready to abandon rock in favor of Beautiful Music. Further, many of the popular artists of the 70s and 80s were baby boomers themselves, and at the age of 35, they still wanted to perform. They did so, quite successfully, finding fans among a new generation of teens while keeping the fans who loved them in the 60s. Such groups as The Who, the Rolling Stones, and Paul McCartney & Wings proved that 40-year-olds could still play rock and roll.

With even better technology that brought about music on compact disc (CD), the 50s and 60s songs now sounded far superior in technical quality to 45s or albums. This made record buyers who hadn't been in a record store in years go back to purchase the CD versions of the songs they had loved when they were growing up. Despite the fact that CDs cost much more than albums, they quickly developed a legion of fans in the 25- to 44-year-old age group, disproving the stereotype about adults buying records only as presents for their kids. CDs became the presents adults bought themselves. Many radio stations also took advantage of how good music sounded on compact disc, and gradually, records were replaced.

Adults nostalgic for their teenage years found Oldies a fun format, and those adults who had grown up with Album Rock soon found they too had a format of their own. As Top-40 music of the 50s and 60s became the oldies of the 80s, so the best-known Album Rock artists of the 60s and 70s became Classic Rock, an Oldies format with album tracks. It too was very successful, mainly on FM and with 25- to 44-year-old males as the target audience. Another major format to evolve came from Black radio and first attained popularity in the late 70s—it was called *Urban* and combined black music with danceable Top-40 songs, as well as including certain long versions (or special mixes) of songs popular in gay clubs and discos. It was up-tempo, yet not rock-oriented, and did especially well with 18- to 34-year-old adults, especially females. Urban was known as excellent party music, since most of it had a good beat, and you could dance to it.

As managers of MOR stations watched all these changes, even the ones that didn't affect their stations directly, many of them were well aware that fixing or changing their music would not be enough to keep their listeners faithful. By the late 70s many people believed that FM was for music—since FM broadcast in stereo, whereas AM did not—and as a result, even the great AM Top-40 stations were finding it difficult to survive. One by one, AM Top-40s slowly fell; even the legendary WABC changed format.

Many MOR stations wondered if it was time to eliminate music from their format. The fact that quite a few did led to the renaming of MOR. Those early days when music was a major part of radio programming had given way to a time when music was only one part of the broadcast day, no more and no less important than "Amos 'n' Andy" or "Ma Perkins" or the latest news.

Now, in some markets, there were so many music-only stations, so many stations playing basically the same songs and chasing the same audience, that MOR split off in several more directions. Those stations that decided to continue playing music (not AC music, but the music beloved by the over-50 audience, with the great vocalists and crooners of the 40s and the pre-rock days) became known as *Nostalgia* stations; some used a syndicated service provided and designed by Al Ham, called "Music of Your Life," and many older listeners who were accustomed to AM but didn't enjoy contemporary music adored this format and loyally supported it.

Those stations that either de-emphasized music or restricted it to one or two specific shows, while concentrating on talk, news, personality, and features came to be known as Full-Service stations. It is interesting that Full-Service became the name of one very narrowly defined type of programming, when in reality, elements of Full-Service could be heard on such Country stations as WSM and were still present when KGU in Honolulu and WBAL in Baltimore stopped playing music entirely and went to a talk-show format. The concept of Full-Service had always included a number of aspects, from entertainment to information, but what held the diverse parts together was the strong local focus and the commitment to being a lot more to the community than just a jukebox.

As the MOR stations of the 50s and 60s positioned themselves, they branched off in several directions. We have already discussed the WBZ and KDKA strategy, but not all stations did this. WTIC in Hartford began putting more talk shows on the air. The station experimented with talk as early as 1954. Prior to that time, WTIC, like many similar stations, had certain programs where interesting guests talked with the show's host; but the absence of tape delays to screen out offensive callers, and the belief that good radio should always be scripted, prevented spontaneous call-ins from listeners. People wrote letters, and sometimes the guest would answer such letters over the air, but few stations allowed any direct interaction to occur.

Since 1935, there had been a network show called "America's Town Meeting of the Air" where studio audience members could ask a question of the guest speakers. Many local stations did their own "Town Meeting" too, but these shows, although often informative and educational, attempted to give a fair and balanced look at a given issue and were a far cry from the confrontational, almost debate-style shows that became popular years later. Still, it had become obvious from the success of person-in-the-street interviews that listeners loved to offer opinions and they also loved hearing themselves and their neighbors on the air.

In 1954, WTIC began an afternoon talk show hosted by DJ Ross Miller and his wife Betty. Another talk show, called "Mikeline," debuted in 1959. As was the tendency back then, talk shows avoided controversy. Most, even with listener call-ins, featured a congenial host and were done in a light, chatty style. Many traditional MOR stations also did well with advice shows, where an expert spoke on a subject and then took questions. Such shows were especially popular on farm stations, which had always had guests to discuss areas such as raising healthier animals or having a better garden; with improvements in technology, listeners could call and have their problems resolved instantly.

Not all early talk shows were big successes. KMA tried one in the early 50s, and it was a dismal failure because of poor planning. Called "Talk of the Town," it was done live at a local cafe. Unfortunately, the regular clientele wasn't especially talkative and the cafe was not centrally located, so there wasn't an influx of new and more loquacious people. The show soon died a merciful death. KMA did try again during the 50s with another talk show, but this one, "KMA Open Line," let the listeners call in to express their opinions, and the results were a lot more interesting.

There were certainly a number of local stations in the 50s that had begun experimenting with call-in shows, but in 1960, the innovative approach of one particular person totally transformed a radio station and helped turn it into a Full-Service legend and a ratings giant. The man was Robert Hyland, and the station was KMOX in St. Louis.

In the early days of radio, being owned by a network or a newspaper had definite benefits: when there was a lack of local programming, the station was given plenty of usable material. Thus WGN (owned by the *Chicago Tribune*), except for a brief hiatus of 2 years during the early 1920s, could rely on the *Tribune* for features, news, sports, and even radio dramas—two of the *Tribune*'s most popular comic strips ("Little Orphan Annie" and "Dick Tracy") became series on WGN during the 30s. Similarly, a station owned by NBC or CBS could depend on a wide variety of shows, with many celebrity performers. As TV achieved dominance during the early 50s, and the important radio shows moved over to TV, suddenly the local affiliates were back to the same problem: filling the time with interesting programs.

KMOX was a CBS station with 50,000 watts. It was profitable; it even had its own orchestra and was able to make do when the CBS network became unable to provide as many programs as it once did. Hyland was KMOX's general manager at that time, and he knew the station had best start doing something unique or it would lose its audience. With KMOX at a crossroad, he felt that simply playing records would not be enough to make the station stand out, so he decided to use some creativity.

Hyland designed and implemented what became the prototype for talk radio as we know it today. The first such program, "At Your Service," began in February of 1960. It was an innovative blend of information and entertainment, where listeners could call in to talk with a variety of important guests, from the mayor to doctors, lawyers, and celebrities. Since Robert Hyland had a long and illustrious career in public service, including active participation on the board of directors of a number of St. Louis cultural and civic organizations, he was well aware of the issues that mattered. He put this knowledge to good use at KMOX, and the station quickly earned a reputation for being in touch with the audience. That quality of knowing exactly what was important to the people of St. Louis, coupled with personalities who demonstrated a deep respect for the listener, made the station's venture into talk radio a great success. Soon, the format was expanded, other talk shows were added, and KMOX was on the way to the fulfillment of its positioning statement: It soon was "The Voice of St. Louis."

KMOX also became known for its ability to get the big-name guests—from presidents to princes, if someone was in the news, chances are, KMOX would find a way to put that person on the air. This aggressive policy, fueled by daily meetings where yesterday's show was rigorously critiqued by the staff and suggestions for improvement made, gave KMOX a standard of excellence that the staff repeatedly attained. Despite coming from the CBS tradition of neutrality in matters of politics, KMOX was the first CBS station to air editorials.

Talk wasn't the only area where KMOX excelled. The station's commitment to service extended to developing an award-winning news team, a morning information show that gave the audience in-depth coverage and analysis 7 days a week, and an intense sports presence that included both play-by-play baseball and football and sports call-in shows. The announcers who did the play-by-play for KMOX over the years reads like a "Who's Who" of sports legends: among them are Jack Buck, Harry Caray, Bob Costas, Joe Garagiola, and Tim McCarver. KMOX did offer some special music-oriented programs, such as a big band show, but in general, what made the station so successful was the combination of service elements it gave the audience. Robert Hyland was ultimately promoted to senior vice president for CBS Radio, and his faith in Full-Service radio has never diminished nor has his belief that listeners want a station that educates, informs and entertains.

KMOX became such a powerhouse that it rose to number one in the ratings and stayed there—for over 20 years! Even in the 80s, supposedly a very trying decade for AM radio, KMOX remained dominant, achieving huge ratings with both the 25- to 54- and 35- to 64-year-old demographics. By the end of the 80s, in fact, KMOX's ratings were in the 20s (the majority of dominant Full-Service stations in other cities typically had ratings that ranged from 10.5 to 16.3), and KMOX was among the most-listened to stations in the entire country—certainly a tribute to the vision of Robert Hyland and the commitment of a dedicated staff who have kept KMOX on top since 1960.

A number of other Full-Service stations followed the KMOX approach, and managed to overcome the AM audience erosion. WGN successfully made the transition into the 70s and beyond with thorough and extensive news coverage, major-league sports, personalities with great warmth and great longevity (including morning man Wally Phillips who had joined the station in the mid-50s and went on to become one of Full-Service's most respected air talents), and other elements for which good Full-Service stations are known. WGN also did features based around a theme, such as a yearly tribute to Benny Goodman, movie reviews, show-business updates, and interviews with interesting guests. Like KMOX, WGN always worked hard to keep the audience involved. WGN still played some music at times: perhaps a program about Broadway show tunes or the music of George Gershwin. Sometimes, there were pleasant contemporary songs too, but like KMOX, WGN had built a solid reputation for news, sports, and public service. Listeners came to WGN to hear the Cubs or the Bears games, but they also knew they could count on WGN to get an important news story first. For many years, WGN has achieved ratings success and is known as a very influential station.

When tracing the history of Full-Service, much attention is often given to those 50,000-watt clear channel stations in large markets; because of their size and signal strength, stations like WLW and WCCO were heard and emulated in numerous other cities. Although it would be wrong to give the impression that Full-Service has enjoyed its greatest success on AM powerhouse stations, it cannot be denied that having 50,000 watts and no interference (back in 1928, the FRC had made this possible for 25 stations; years later, with space allocations at a premium, it proved to be an unpopular decision) has been a great help for these stations, which also include WBT, WTIC, KMOX, and WSB.

Full-Service radio can and does succeed in markets of all sizes, from major to tiny, but, to do this format well, stations need both money and patience. Like All News, Full-Service can be expensive because in-depth local coverage can require a larger staff than a station that just plays music would need. Also, creating an image of reliability requires constant public contact, good equipment for doing actualities and remote broadcasts, and ongoing publicity so that people in the community are aware of the station. As for patience, adults who have a favorite station are unlikely to switch to another immediately; they need to be won over. Teens, for example, are considered more fickle in their choice of stations. They may prefer one station for a while, but if another appears and claims to play more music or have bigger contests, teens will sample that station.

Attracting adults, especially older adults, is a more challenging task, since adults tend to become accustomed to a given station (usually because of its personalities or its unique features), and they are reticent to try something different. Part of the reason adults find Full-Service stations so comfortable is that sense of stability. Where Top-40 stations would frequently change entire air staffs, that was seldom true with Full-Service, and Full-Service announcers not only stayed at the same station, they lived in the area, belonged to local civic groups, sent their kids to the local schools, and worked hard to promote the station as one big, happy family.

So while having legendary call letters and a strong signal are beneficial, nothing can save a Full-Service station if it isn't aware of what its audience wants. Many of the program directors I interviewed for this book observed that listeners' tastes have changed greatly over the past few years with regard to what issues are now acceptable to discuss. Subjects that were taboo as recently as 10 years ago are now totally safe, but these program directors also noted that a station must know the limits and boundaries too. Even the most controversial topic (one that I recall is an appearance by several lesbian nuns on a talk show in a *very* Catholic city) can be handled professionally, without resorting to sensationalism. Full-Service stations seldom shy away from touchy subjects anymore, but because the image of this format is family-oriented, great effort is made to avoid double-entendres, questionable language, or the techniques the shock-jocks might use. Full-Service promises to keep the listeners informed, but it doesn't shout at the audience or insult its intelligence.

It is also important, the program directors told me, to know what the audience wants, rather than assuming that what they liked last year works fine now, or what people in New York care about will also interest people in Cedar Rapids, Iowa. True, there are some universal issues, but stations that want to stay on top research their audience often enough to know what issues are important to them now.

WCCO is a good example of changing with the times: until 1943, the station offered little local news, relying mainly on its network, CBS, but as people demanded more local coverage, WCCO committed itself to getting the job done. Once

WCCO had established itself as the authority for local news, it never stopped promoting that position. When major-league baseball came to the Twin Cities, WCCO was there to carry the games. When an issue that affected Minnesota's farmers occurred, WCCO had reporters available immediately to both cover and clarify the story. WCCO too built a morning show with intense information coupled with a very humorous pair of announcers—Roger Erickson and Charlie Boone had been entertaining Minnesotans for 30 years as this book went to press. WCCO never rested on its past success; it kept building new successes and winning new audience; it is a perennial ratings leader.

Just as it would be wrong to imply that only AM stations with 50,000 watts, large markets, and larger budgets remained on top with Full-Service, it would also be wrong to say that Full-Service succeeds only at heritage stations. Yes, the KMOXs, KDKAs and WBZs have the advantage of a set of well-known and well-respected call letters, but even in the days of AM audience erosion, there were new Full-Service stations going on the air and earning the audience's approval.

One very interesting station is KRVN in Lexington, Nebraska. KRVN didn't go on the air until 1951, from a town with a population of roughly 7000. What is unique about KRVN is its owners: all 4000 of them. KRVN is owned by a group of area farmers and ranchers, who formed the Nebraska Rural Radio Association (NRRA) in 1949. When KRVN first went on the air, it operated only during daytime hours. Today, it is a full-time station, and it serves listeners in both Nebraska and Kansas, as well as parts of three other states. The station isn't all farm news: it offers sports (both college and professional), has a sizeable commitment to national and international news, and plays some music (mostly Country).

General manager Eric Brown says the key to the station's popularity is that "we take care of the listener. If you asked our audience to describe the station, they'd use words like 'reliable' and 'trustworthy.'" KRVN found a definite niche: serving the agricultural industry. Farmers felt existing stations didn't address their needs. KRVN superserves them with a large number of up-to-the-minute weather reports, nearly 100 farm-oriented special programs, the latest market reports, and coverage of any meetings that impact on farmers and ranchers. Further, KRVN serves as an electronic newsletter, enabling various farm organizations to keep in touch and publicize what they are doing. KRVN may be small in terms of market size, but its attitude is to keep the listeners and the retail clients satisfied. The station even does research to anticipate what new features KRVN ought to carry. Eric Brown used this research in the past to add more national news, as it became apparent that Nebraska farmers wanted to know what was happening in other cities besides their own. The station also has contests, sending winners to Kansas City with their friends to see a major-league baseball game or giving Country-music lovers the chance to see the Opry in Nashville. KRVN calls itself "The Rural Voice of Nebraska," and since its earliest days, it has been a lifeline for farmers and ranchers and a financial success for its owners (who reinvest the profits to further improve the station).

In South Dakota, several successful Full-Service stations have been owned and operated by women. Sylvia Henkin was president of KSOO in Sioux Falls, and later chairman of the board, until the station was sold in the late 80s; the station was founded by the Henkin family in 1926. KSOO's slogan is "KSOO, When You Need to Know," which describes its approach as the market's news and information authority. KSOO has a larger news staff than its competitors; in addition to extensive local coverage, KSOO also offers agricultural and business updates on a regular basis. At one point, KSOO changed its music to Country, but when it became obvious that only a vocal minority wanted Country, the station changed back to AC. KSOO is yet another Full-Service with a well-established morning show: host Wayne Pritchard was celebrating his thirtieth anniversary as this book went to press. When Sioux Falls was awarded a Continental Basketball Association (CBA) franchise, KSOO was right there to broadcast the games. The station has also done a lot to raise money for organizations that help the retarded and the handicapped.

Meanwhile, in Rapid City, Helen Duhamel is the woman who turned KOTA around. When she acquired the station in 1954, it was on the verge of bankruptcy. Today, not only is KOTA Radio alive and well but so is the TV station she bought in 1955 (it became the first TV station in western South Dakota). Like KSOO, KOTA Radio has earned a reputation as the best source for credible news; the station has become known for its ability to get the important stories first. Rapid City also has a CBA team, and KOTA Radio broadcasts the games; the station is also a major booster of most events that take place in the area. For many years, KOTA was a traditional MOR, with block programming and an older audience. Under the leadership of Helen Duhamel's son Bill, the station modernized, moved to AC music, shortened some of the excessively long talk features, and designed informational programs to address the needs of the 35- to 44-year-olds. With a better signal (5000 watts, up from the 250 it once had) and better programming, KOTA succeeded.

Among the best examples of doing Full-Service well in a smaller market is the award-winning Cedar Rapids, Iowa, station, WMT. This station has been so profitable, in fact, that a group of nine current and former WMT employees were able to purchase the station themselves in 1986—for $8.1 million! Over the years, WMT has been regarded as a good neighbor and a friend to the people of Cedar Rapids: the station is very willing to be a cheerleader on behalf of locally grown products, and it gives awards to good citizens. WMT is known for its continuous efforts on behalf of the community. Some of its projects have included fund-raising for Camp Courageous (a camp for the physically and mentally handicapped); designing innovative public service programs to combat drunk driving; creating a campaign to promote farm safety; and "Care & Share," which collects Christmas gifts for the needy. WMT has its own meteorologist; it also has a farm director who travels all over the world gathering information about the latest exports and any other international news that will keep local farmers up to date. WMT also has an opulent mobile studio for remotes and its own hot-air balloon. With a blend of AC music, established air personalities, talk shows, farm news, public service, and ongoing promotions (such as the Lawn, Garden & Home Exposition, or cruises on the Mississippi River), WMT maintains its position as "The Voice of Iowa." If AMs in other markets are having problems, there is certainly no sign of it in Cedar Rapids, where WMT events draw huge audiences.

Whether in large markets like St. Louis or small markets like Lexington, Nebraska, there are many Full-Service stations that have become adept at making the format fit the changing needs of the audience. Since the earliest example of Full-Service at KDKA, the format has proved to be very flexible. It may be called Variety or MOR or Nostalgia, but by any name, Full-Service continues to be a remarkably durable format.

6
▼ Full-Service Adapts
▼ to the Future
▼
▼
▼

There seem to be a few traits virtually every successful Full-Service station has in common. One is an excellent morning show, with an announcer who exemplifies stability and longevity. At WMAL in Washington D.C., Frank Harden and Jackson Weaver began doing mornings in 1960 and were still in command 30 years later. In Boston, a market with a number of experienced morning show hosts, WHDH (which was Full-Service until it switched to Talk in the late 1980s) has a history of well-known announcers, among whom is the critically acclaimed Jess Cain; over at WBZ, it was Carl DeSuze for many years, and then Dave Maynard (Maynard is best known for some very creative TV commercials in which he is seen in a number of dangerous situations, such as in the ring with boxer Marvin Hagler, confronting a tiger, or trying to ski jump). WGN has Wally Phillips, WTIC has Bob Steele, several generations of John Gambling have been entertaining New York on WOR. Even in the small markets, there are legends who have been on the air for years.

Another common trait at successful Full-Service stations is a willingness to be visible. WMT is not the only station that spent money on a beautiful, state-of-the-art mobile studio. KDKA's is called the Radio Rainbow Machine and has the slogan "Pittsburgh: Some Place Special" prominently displayed. As most operators of Full-Service stations have acknowledged, it can be an expensive format to do well, but people who attend station events remember the station by the caliber of its equipment. Stations like WBZ, KMOX, and WCCO (whose van says "Real Radio WCCO") believe in putting forth a good image.

Another trait that successful Full-Service stations possess is constant dedication to the community. WMAL has raised funds for numerous D.C. area charities including both the Boys and the Girls Clubs, the Leukemia Society, and the Children's Hospital National Medical Center. KMOX supports Boys Town of Missouri and Food for the Needy. WHAS in Louisville is known for helping crippled children through the "WHAS Crusade for Children."

Full-Service stations do more than raise funds for major charities. They also reach out to individuals in crisis, such as the time when WIBC in Indianapolis heard about some families who had lost everything in a fire, or KOTA learned of a little girl whose family didn't have enough money for the kidney transplant she needed. Full-Service stations over the years have become a friend to the audience: thanks to the efforts of these stations, deserving schools have gotten computers, shut-ins have received flowers on their birthdays, and countless people have been reunited with lost pets.

In fact, most Full-Service stations (including the ones who have become associated with one major charitable appeal such as the March of Dimes or United Way) are constantly doing public-service events. WHAS is one of the stations that has a softball team, which plays benefit games for various charities. At times, Full-Service seems almost old-fashioned or sentimental, wishing certain listeners a happy anniversary or praising someone for being especially civic-minded; but the recipients of this attention deeply appreciate it. It's all part of making listeners feel like members of a family.

In looking at Full-Service stations, it is easy to generalize and say they all have strong news images and a commitment to service, but each station has its own unique way of serving. Although the majority of Full-Service stations have extensive sports coverage, be it professional or college, a few are doing fine without any large sports commitment. WBZ in Boston used to broadcast many sports events, but by the late 80s, that had diminished greatly. Yet, despite the big teams being on other stations, WBZ's ratings did not suffer—in fact, they grew. WBZ became known for other elements: the most accurate weather, traffic reports from the helicopter, high-profile announcers, and locally produced evening talk shows. WBZ positioned this local talk directly against its competitors, who used syndicated programs; thus, if a listener wanted to talk about a Boston issue, only WBZ made this possible.

Not all Full-Service stations have a lot of talk shows, however. Some restrict call-in shows to mainly nights and weekends. Some, especially in smaller markets where good local talk hosts are difficult to find, rely on syndication or network talk shows. WTIC used to do much more talk in the 60s than in the 80s. Sports talk seems to be successful in many places, and WTIC is among the stations with a call-in sports program, to complement its own sports coverage (Boston Red Sox baseball and Hartford Whalers hockey).

WTIC built its reputation on its news, weather, and other information elements—for years, it used the slogan "WTIC, the Pulse of New England." WTIC still plays music and isn't afraid to play a new record that fits the station's contemporary sound. However, WTIC knows how to promote itself in a way that will be noticed. The station has used billboards, for example; the WTIC billboards light up and describe what is on the air right now, with an invitation to tune in. Like many Full-Service stations, WTIC has a full-time promotions director to help plan upcoming events and publicize the station's benefits.

KDKA is another station that plays more music than many Full-Service stations. It too has limited talk shows, mostly in the evening. Like WBZ, KDKA is known for up-to-the-minute traffic reports (which are crucial in large cities where many people listen in their car on the way to or from work), and like WBZ, KDKA is a blend of music and information during the day, with entertaining announcers. KDKA has been a sports leader for years, but the station doesn't rely on sports alone. One unique call-in show that KDKA has is on Sunday nights, when a priest moderates a call-in show that discusses ethical and moral issues of the day.

In Cincinnati, WLW has always been known as an innovator, and throughout the years, the station has continued to offer interviews with the biggest celebrities in movies, music, and politics. Like other Full-Service giants however, WLW has had to constantly reevaluate what each new generation of listeners wants. The key has been attracting new audience to replace the older demographics. WLW does this not only with sports coverage (Cincinnati Reds baseball and Xavier College basketball) but with more issues-oriented talk, including subjects that might have been considered inappropriate a few years ago. WLW's research has shown that 60% of the audience is male, so the station does well with its sports call-in show each night.

WLW's musical approach is somewhat different from most Full-Service stations: although WLW's music isn't rock, it also isn't traditional MOR. The station plays songs that the 35- to 54-year-old males would like, rather than the usual soft-AC blend of mellow ballads. (In fact, on one talk show, the subject was the lyrics to current rock hits.)

WLW also has a unique element to go along with its strong news and information package: during the 80s, afternoons were much more amusing, thanks to the award-winning DJ Gary Burbank, who offered innovative comedy skits featuring his own cast of characters. Not since the days of the vaudeville comedians has a station devoted so much energy to making people laugh.

On a more serious note, WLW has been the only station in the area with a traffic helicopter. The station also has a determination to keep its programming relevant to listeners under 40 years old, even those who didn't listen much to AM in the past.

One especially interesting success story involves a station that at one time had a rather controversial image, yet transcended it to become one of Full-Service's most respected stations. WJR in Detroit, long known as "The Goodwill Station" and "The Great Voice of the Great Lakes," once had the dubious distinction of being the radio home of Father Coughlin, the extremely bigoted priest who used radio to gain a wider audience for his views. Unfortunately, in the 1930s, one man who agreed with Father Coughlin's message was WJR's owner, George Richards.

Mr. Richards had many famous and influential friends who liked him in spite of his prejudices, but his control at WJR (and the other stations he owned) had some rather negative effects. He had very pronounced views, for example, especially with regard to Jews (whom he hated) and any political figures who didn't match his standards of patriotism. He sent memos to his news directors, ordering them to say nothing positive about President or Mrs. Roosevelt. He also gave similar dictates about other government officials whom he thought were communists. News directors who protested were fired: at one of his stations, he had seven news directors in 3 years.

He was ultimately investigated by the FCC, but his license was never revoked. WJR was, even then, very profitable and had a large audience. Richards had another side that may have somewhat balanced off his tyrannical management style: he was known to be very generous to the people who stayed with him; he paid them well and was loyal to them. Thus, when other radio stations lost most of their best people to TV, the majority of the stars at WJR stayed there.

Over the years, many celebrities performed at WJR's studios, including Jackie Gleason and Arthur Godfrey. Later, it would be Barbra Streisand and Bette Midler. WJR, like many Full-Service stations, had established itself as *the* place for an up-and-coming star to get exposure; once these stars did become famous, they often returned to the station to perform.

George Richards, for all his personal biases, understood entertainment. He had made his fortune by selling cars, and he knew how to put on a show for the customers. He carried this flair into running WJR. He was proud of the station; he had once been an advertiser on WJR. Now that he owned it, he was just as devoted to it. He was also determined to make the station a household word. WJR's strategy entailed never reacting to other stations. WJR was unique; it offered something for everyone, but the questions about the station's slanting of the news lingered on. A battle to revoke George Richards' licenses had resumed when suddenly he died.

In order to save the stations he had owned, his widow signed an agreement in 1950, promising that there would never again be any news-slanting or propagandizing. WJR was eventually bought by ABC (later Capital Cities) and established an excellent reputation for fairness and accuracy in news reporting.

Working hard on the service elements for which Full-Service is known, WJR has become an institution in Detroit, a station known for sports (Tigers baseball especially), traffic and weather reports, interesting special features, a mobile studio that is constantly out doing remotes, and a tradition of representing everything important that goes on in the area. WJR has a history of attracting celebrities, and it also gives the audience an opportunity to talk with the mayor (who has even filled in on the morning show at times) or the governor. Although WJR no longer slants the news, it isn't afraid to uncover corruption or scandal, through its award-winning investigative team. WJR does play some music, but as is the case with many Full-Service stations, it is best known as an information source and has continually earned the loyalty of its target audience, adults 40 years old and over. In essence, WJR has succeeded because it has marketed itself in a very positive fashion (using TV commercials and billboards to spread awareness of the station's benefits) and has aggressively pursued exciting and interesting guests, to go along with a very experienced air staff. WJR's logo says it best: "WJR Stands For Detroit."

In Washington D.C., the Full-Service heritage station is WMAL, the initials of which stand for M. A. Leese, a local optometrist who first put the station on the air in October of 1925. From its early days, when it only broadcast 3 nights a week, WMAL grew steadily, first as a CBS-network affiliate during the late 20s (when the station only had 500 watts), then during the 30s as an NBC affiliate, and finally, into the 40s, with a power increase to 5000 watts and a new affiliation with ABC.

Today, WMAL maintains that ABC (now Capital Cities) affiliation, and the station continued its growth by becoming Washington's first AM-stereo station in

1982. In fact, WMAL has numerous firsts, including being the first area station to broadcast airborne traffic reports. WMAL's positioning is expressed in its slogan : "WMAL—Depend On It."

The station may not have 50,000 watts, but it has an innovative way of making people remember it, with some unique promotions. One successful promotion involved station personnel appearing every Thursday morning at Metro stops (the Metro is Washington's public transportation) to hand out free coffee and doughnuts to people on their way to work; on every coffee cup and every napkin was the WMAL logo. WMAL has also used bus cards and TV commercials to promote itself, but the station is best known for the events it sponsors, such as an annual Christmas Eve free concert which WMAL broadcasts live from the Kennedy Center. In addition to traditional Christmas music, the concert features major celebrity entertainers. Morning legends Harden & Weaver have held yearly golf tournaments for charity since 1970.

WMAL is highly visible in the community. The station is the voice of professional football, with Washington Redskins games; and, of course, there is a successful sports talk show too. WMAL also prides itself on the celebrity guests it has interviewed, as well as having some of the best-known personality announcers in the market. WMAL also has a highly respected and award-winning news team; the station has an image of reliability, and its stature hasn't been affected by the market's very suc-cessful All News station, WTOP.

In Albany-Schenectady, New York, another heritage station has undergone several transitions. WGY traces its beginnings back to 1922, and over the years, it has established itself as the market's news leader; WGY used to refer to itself as "a Tradition of Information." The station was an MOR for a long time, playing mainly music from the pre-rock era, but like KDKA and WBZ, WGY saw its audience aging and gradually moved to a more contemporary sound, with a heavy emphasis on oldies and features like "Class Reunion," where a particular year was recalled, and hits from that year were played.

During the 1980s, as younger listeners continued to choose FM, WGY de-emphasized music and concentrated more on talk, news, and special features. Research the station did showed that the WGY audience still wanted some music and didn't want extended talk blocks. So WGY created afternoon *infotainment*, a magazine-style format with some music and segments on health, finances, movies, and, of course, news, weather, and traffic.

The station also had a history of very popular evening talk shows; WGY had not carried much sports over the years, becoming best-known for its personality announcers and its thought-provoking call-in shows.

WGY still has one unresolved problem though, something facing many medium-market stations. A good local talk show can get listeners, but it is very expensive to do well. (Finding interesting guests can be time-consuming, and a producer is often necessary.) Stations faced with shrinking advertising revenues may have to cut costs in the future. For now, WGY just wants to entertain and inform.

WIBC in Indianapolis was once a struggling Top-40 station; in its several decades of Full-Service, it has found the perfect niche. WIBC has a large news team; it also carries pro football. WIBC doesn't have many talk shows, but it does have a very vocal audience which isn't shy about expressing likes and dislikes. WIBC is known for its constant involvement with its market, yet the station's vice president–general manager, Roy Cooper, says, "We don't seek headlines. We just provide good radio." Positioning itself as "The Voice of News for Indiana," WIBC was also the first station in the market to use direct mail to promote itself.

Some stations in smaller markets have been doing Full-Service for as long as the big-name stations like WCCO and KDKA; they are often called *community stations* because they serve one very specific local area. WGCH in Greenwich, Connecticut, is such a station. Located less than an hour from New York City, Greenwich easily receives most of New York's signals, yet WGCH has still become successful because New York stations seldom give detailed coverage to the distant suburbs.

Although many Greenwich residents work in New York, they love their hometown and are very involved with it. WGCH has the advantage of serving a city of 60,000 people; it is an affluent and very educated community. News and information are very important to these people, and only WGCH can give them the in-depth local reporting they can't hear anywhere else.

Dennis Jackson, who was general manager of WGCH before leaving to purchase another community station, WREF in Ridgefield, Connecticut, recalls, "Greenwich is a perfect place to do Full-Service, because the people have such a spirit of volunteerism. So we could reflect on what people were doing and involve them in the station. People like to hear themselves and their neighbors on the air. That's why we used the slogan 'Keeping You in Touch with Your Community.'"

WGCH has a very thorough and visible news staff, and the station has encouraged local political figures to be on the air, answering questions from the audience. Like many community stations, WGCH has continued to provide as complete (if not more complete) reporting of political events as any New York station, and is also visible in the community with a variety of charitable activities. Under subsequent managers, WGCH has continued to do what it does best: news, information, features, and talk shows, but always oriented to Greenwich.

In Canada, CKAC is worth discussing because it was such a trail-blazing station, and it did have a relationship with the U.S. networks for a while. CKAC's innovative efforts on behalf of French-Canada led to its being the flagship of a French news network, which serves stations across the country. CKAC has always reached out to its audience, from its earliest days on the air when it was first to broadcast the daily mass (a major service for its largely Catholic audience). As with U.S. Full-Service stations, CKAC developed a reputation for getting the interviews with the biggest celebrities. When baseball came to Montreal, there was CKAC to bring the play-by-play of the Expos games, in addition to the Montreal Canadiens hockey games it had carried for years. CKAC was not afraid to editorialize nor to talk about the difficult issues, even in a conservative city. When city planners began redesigning the city's highways, CKAC immediately upgraded and improved its traffic reports. CKAC still plays some music, but as with its counterparts in the United States, the station has moved more towards talk and features over the past decade. CKAC also has the same problem that many AM stations face—even though Canada's regulating commission, the CRTC, has made certain AM remains viable, younger listeners have still switched over to FM. Thus, CKAC, with its news and talk shows and traffic from its airplane, still has an audience whose median age is 45 years, and the challenge is to attract younger listeners for something more than just sports.

In another important Canadian market, Toronto, the situation is similar. CFRB was one of Toronto's first stations and has many years of service. For a long time, CFRB remained a traditional MOR station, with lots of block programming. The morning host, Wally Crouter, had been there for over 40 years, the station had a huge signal that blanketed southern Ontario, and the news staff featured the commentaries of Gordon Sinclair (whose pro-United States editorial "The Americans" was set to music and turned into a surprise hit record in 1974, with a cover version by another Canadian newsperson, Byron MacGregor of CKLW, Windsor, going to #4 on the U.S. charts!).

CFRB was very stable for many years, in a city with so few problems that early attempts to do issues-oriented talk shows failed: the Toronto audience felt life was basically good, and few listeners called in. The 80s, however, was a decade of societal change everywhere, including Toronto, and suddenly, the newspapers were writing of urban crime, drugs, and the widening gap between the rich and the poor. Now, more people wanted to express their views, and radio stations, CFRB among them, adjusted accordingly. CFRB was "Ontario's Authoritative News Voice" as well as "Reliable Radio." As life in Toronto grew more complex, CFRB was there to cover it accordingly, becoming a much more issues-driven station. CFRB hasn't carried much sports: the niche it carved out was a solid information-oriented station, keeping people up to date, as well as entertaining them with lighter fare, such as movie reviews or the latest happenings in show business.

Meanwhile, about an hour away from Toronto, a community station, CHUC in Cobourg, is also redefining what today's audience expects from radio. In the 50s, like many small stations in both the United States and Canada, CHUC didn't have a lot of competition. Its niche was mainly that it was there. With TV still not a factor, and FM not yet established, stations like CHUC had a captive audience; they were the best way to find out what was happening nationally as well as locally. As for programming, CHUC was all over the road—Country music in the morning, traditional MOR during the day, including a talk show, back to Country at night, and some rock and roll on the weekends. The station did interviews with people on the street, broadcast high school glee club recitals, and offered a well-intentioned but very inconsistent form of radio, similar to how it was done in the 30s.

When there weren't many other choices, it may not have been a bad idea to be all things to all people; but as soon as more stations, both radio and TV, appeared, listeners became more selective, and community stations like CHUC suddenly found they needed a programming philosophy. To help them become more consistent, many stations (CHUC among them) hired a consultant, which had never been necessary in smaller markets previously. CHUC also had the benefit of a new owner and astute management, and along with some local research, the staff was able to make the station more contemporary and give it the focus it had lacked.

Few stations in either the United States or Canada today have the luxury of being the only game in town; as a result, listeners expect a smoother and more professional sound even in smaller markets. This can certainly give small-market announcers a standard of excellence to strive for, but, unfortunately, it has also made some owners throw up their hands in despair and decide their little station can't compete with the bigger ones, leading to satellite formats or simulcasting of whatever their FM is doing.

In CHUC's case, the station didn't give up; it concentrated on serving its community effectively. Like WGCH in Greenwich, which didn't try to be a clone of a New York station, CHUC didn't try to become a Toronto station, although its news coverage would include any important stories from there. CHUC made the transition into a modern Full-Service station, however, with the emphasis on being the information source for the entire county, offering in-depth coverage of local issues, as well as editorial commentary. The music is AC with a good variety of oldies, and the target audience is typically 35 years old and over.

Fortunately for both Full-Service and AM, not all managers of small-market stations abandoned live radio, but the 80s certainly brought the issue to the forefront, as some community stations went dark, and others decided to become part of a satellite network. Although satellites have been a blessing in some ways (they are cost-effective and keep the station on the air and professional-sounding in markets where good talent is hard to find), they have also been seen by some as a last resort.

Local radio on AM has been in crisis in some small markets, especially those where the economy has been on a downturn, or in small markets that exist in close proximity to a large market. Many agencies and sponsors, their budgets stretched because of the ever-increasing number of media choices (AM, FM, free TV, cable TV, newspapers, magazines, etc.), began eliminating small-market radio stations from their buys, concentrating on the larger stations, in the belief that people in small markets would be likely to listen to the big-city stations more than to local radio.

Whether or not this is true can be debated, but the end result was that a station in Boston would get the buy, whereas a station 70 miles away on Cape Cod might be bypassed. With ad revenues more difficult to obtain and with the day-to-day cost of running a station (salaries, music licenses, equipment repairs, telephone and electric bills, office rent, etc.) steadily rising, those AM stations that were committed to doing Full-Service found it even more challenging.

However, there were stations which didn't switch over to a satellite or change to an easier format, and there are still small-market stations which serve a specific local area and intend to continue doing so. Some of these are helped by an FM sister station which is financially successful, but others (like both WGCH and CHUC) are stand-alone AMs, determined to give their local audience the attention it deserves. For many of these stations, the format they choose is Full-Service.

When I interviewed Vice President-General Manager Vern Falk of WFAW, Fort Atkinson, Wisconsin, he jokingly remarked that with all the predictions about the demise of AM radio, maybe by next year his station wouldn't be around. Then he turned serious and talked proudly about how WFAW has overcome quite a few obstacles and managed to succeed.

For one, Fort Atkinson is about 30 miles from a much larger market (Madison), so WFAW's listeners have many other stations to choose from. Also, until 1989, WFAW was a daytime-only station. In a smaller market, there aren't the resources to pay big-name talent, so WFAW's announcers, while hard-working, sometimes lack the polish of those in Madison. What WFAW does have is dedication. Fort Atkinson itself has approximately 10,000 residents, and WFAW also serves surrounding towns. Like many community stations, WFAW's niche is that it offers more local news than the Madison stations do.

WFAW has a very issues-oriented midday talk show, and it isn't afraid to discuss a controversial matter: when a new plant was about to open in the area, the show's host asked a company executive about how much pollution the plant might cause. The station has done remote broadcasts from area schools, discussing drug use among young people and how to prevent it, and, with many farmers in the listening audience, WFAW has a strong commitment to farm news. The station lets people know who gave birth; it also does obituaries.

Although big city stations might find such features inappropriate, people who live in closely knit communities find them informational. In fact, WFAW refers to itself as "Information 94" (its dial position is 940 AM). WFAW has an aggressive sales staff, and everything that can be sold, is. The good side of that is the station is financially viable. The bad side, from a programming standpoint, is there is considerable commercial clutter—as much as *18* minutes of commercials each hour. Falk acknowledges that this can be a tune-out and is looking at ways to reduce some of the clutter while still keeping WFAW profitable. For all those people who want to know what's happening in their hometown, WFAW is the best place to hear about it.

WTAG in Worcester, Massachusetts is another successful AM that operates not that far away from a much larger market (Boston, 45 miles away). WTAG has made itself very visible over the years, covering a market that has undergone considerable growth. WTAG's history goes as far back as 1924, in fact. It was owned by the *Worcester Telegram & Gazette* (from whence the initials WTAG) for many years, which certainly helped the station establish a strong news image. Although the newspaper ultimately sold WTAG in 1987, the station continued to maintain that image.

WTAG was one of the original NBC affiliates and used to air many of the great radio dramas and comedies during radio's golden age. The station has always had the largest news staff in the market and has been there for every major celebrity or political figure who came to town. WTAG promotes itself by helping the community: it was the first station in central Massachusetts to have a van that aids motorists in distress; in addition to helping the driver's car get started, the van's operator, who is a mechanic, also gives the person a promotional gift with WTAG's call letters on it. WTAG has traffic reports, carries Red Sox baseball, and is considered the authoritative voice for school closings. The station admittedly has an older audience, but it also has great credibility and is a reliable resource for every major event in Worcester.

The key to survival for AM Full-Service stations seems to be carving out a unique position in the market, doing something no other stations do (or doing something that others do, but doing it much more effectively). That uniqueness can manifest itself through a very special personality (such as WSB's legendary midday host Ludlow Porch; humorist, trivia expert, and author, his shows became known for their unpredictable topics of discussion). Other times it shows up in useful information, such as the programs stations like KMOX and KDKA offer, where experts answer questions about major concerns the listeners have: caring for aged parents, which prescription medications are most likely to have side effects, what to do about a bad credit report, or how safe is the stock market. At some stations, it's simply being the station that broadcasts the big sporting events; at others, it's having the most interesting sports talk, with a host who can stir up the fans. Some stations do it with traffic reports, the best meteorologist, controversial talk shows, or editorials that tackle the tough issues. Some offer features that can't be heard anywhere else: old radio dramas brought back for a new generation, a Saturday night Oldies show with requests and dedications, or a Big Band tribute with all the great memories from the Golden Age of Radio. Some use comedians, others use respected news commentators. For some, their uniqueness is in their community service, the many hours they spend raising money for worthy causes and publicizing upcoming charitable events. Some stations still have the older programs, such as "Swap Shop," where listeners can buy, sell, or trade items. Others are seeking new and innovative ways to bring a younger demographic to Full-Service. Some are AM-stereo; some have a van and a helicopter; some just have a small staff who love their hometown and aren't afraid to say so.

As a way of expressing appreciation for the many ways that local stations serve their community, the National Association of Broadcasters (NAB) created the Crystal Radio Awards in 1987. The NAB states that the purpose of these awards is to pay tribute to the way radio stations have improved the quality of life in their local communities. There are four basic categories on which entrants are judged: consistent local programming and coverage; interaction with listeners, community groups, and businesses; public-service campaigns; and community leadership and involvement by station staff.

It should come as no surprise that a large number of Crystal Award winners are Full-Service stations. In addition to the big names like KMOX or WMT, there are also winners from community stations like KSEN in Shelby, Montana, which distinguished itself during a major winter storm by being the one link residents of the area had with the outside world during prolonged power outages and impassable road conditions. KSEN's one full-time newsperson kept thousands of people up to date on the storm's progress and when repairs would be made, while station staff provided reassurance to anxious listeners who had no other way of knowing what was happening.

Other winners came from important secondary markets, such as WCTC in New Brunswick, New Jersey, which calls itself "Central New Jersey's Information Source." The station was honored for raising $110,000 in 1989 for the March of Dimes, creating a series of historical vignettes saluting the 300-year anniversary of Somerset County, and helping the audience better understand local politics by inviting all the candidates be on the air prior to election day to field questions from the listeners.

The Crystal Awards are an excellent way of spotlighting the efforts of stations in markets of all sizes. Although station managers don't devote themselves to their community just to win awards, it is still an exciting and gratifying moment each year at the NAB's Radio Convention when the winners are announced and the awards are presented before a large group of appreciative broadcasters from all over the world.

What makes ceremonies like the Crystal Awards even more meaningful is the fact that since deregulation, doing a specific amount of public service is no longer mandatory. Years ago, part of license renewal involved doing *ascertainments*, a process where community leaders had to be interviewed so that they could express to the station what issues they felt needed to be addressed. Some stations did the bare minimum of public service, while others buried such shows at 5 A.M., since they believed these shows were not very interesting to the average person. Thus, it is all the more remarkable that there are so many stations where public service is not considered a burden or a bore. True, in order to get a license renewed even since deregulation, stations must demonstrate that they have served the community, but how that service should be performed is currently left up to each station.

An FCC inspector who happens to be in the area, or any member of the public, can request to see a station's public file, and it's a wise station which keeps an up-to-date public file, deregulation or not. The reason for the public file is to document exactly what the station has been doing for the community and what issues it has addressed. Playing the hits is not enough to get a license renewed. In the old days, stations were warned that making a profit and keeping advertisers happy wasn't what having a license was all about; even now, stations are still expected to operate in the public interest. In the public file, there should be copies of letters listeners have sent, a list of what public-service programs have been run and what issues these programs addressed (as well as any other pertinent information about how the station addressed the needs of its community), and legal papers such as ownership reports. The programs and issues list should be updated quarterly.

When I think of Full-Service, I think of the immediacy with which it addresses public service. I think of KNBR in San Francisco, a 50,000-watt heritage station that has served the Bay Area since 1922, and a station that has all the elements typical of large-market Full-Service: a famous morning team (Frank Dill and Mike Cleary), Oakland A's baseball, and a variety of talk shows to complement its news and information image. KNBR could easily sit back and point to its achievements from past years. One night, I was watching the late-night news on CNN, and there was a story about a little boy who had cancer and desperately needed a donor for a bone-marrow transplant, and his time was running out with no suitable donor having been found. Then, I saw it: a local radio station, KNBR, was setting up a booth and publicizing the need for potential donors. I said to myself, "Isn't that what you'd expect from a Full-Service station?" It is exactly that sort of compassion, that willingness to reach out to individuals in the community, that makes Full-Service radio so special. Once more, a Full-Service station had demonstrated what it means to broadcast in the public interest.

Full-Service has undergone many changes since it began, and it is still experiencing more change. Some media watchers are predicting the end of this format; others say it will move over to FM. In the next chapter, we will examine some methods for making sure a Full-Service station stays in touch with the audience and doesn't let itself become outdated.

7
How To Do Full-Service: The Right Research

KSSK in Honolulu is not a Full-Service station, yet, except for the market's All News and News/Talk stations, nobody gives more information. KSSK does whatever it takes to keep listeners informed: during a major rain storm, the station suspended its regular programming to let people know the latest road conditions, where the storm was headed next, and how residents with storm-related problems could get assistance.

KSSK has personality announcers who enjoy entertaining the audience, and the station plays some great oldies. There are no talk shows per se, but the announcers discuss local issues and take calls from listeners. There is also a consumer advocate who responds to listeners' complaints. People trust KSSK and have done so for many years, yet according to the station's president and general manager, Earl McDaniel, "You can't really put a label on what we do; we're so many different things. But we always keep it local." So is KSSK a Full-Service station after all?

How about WBAL, a Crystal Award winner, honored in 1988 for doing over 200 public service events? WBAL used to be a traditional MOR until it switched to Talk radio in the 80s. Yet, even though it no longer plays music, it still has Orioles baseball, a well-known and very entertaining morning show, and the aforementioned major commitment to serving the community.

It's not just AM stations that do a lot for their local area: on the FM band there are a number of stations that have also won Crystal awards, such as WTLC-FM, an Urban station in Indianapolis which was honored in 1989 for its excellence in broadcast journalism, issues-oriented talk shows, and a public affairs program that gives the audience an opportunity to hear from their elected officials.

Some media magazines use the terms *Full-Service* and *Adult Contemporary* interchangeably. Others write about the format as if only people over 50 years old listen to it, or as if it's really News/Talk radio in disguise. As we have noted in previous chapters, even those stations that do identify themselves as Full-Service run the gamut from just about all talk and features (like KMOX) to some talk and features (WBZ) to very little talk, some features, and some music (CHUC).

We have discussed the elements nearly all Full-Service stations have, such as a stable air staff with roots in the community (at WHO in Des Moines, the award-winning Farm Service Department has members with 36 and 40 years of experience, plus one newcomer who has 9); a major news commitment; emphasis on weather and/or traffic reporting; and an image of extensive public service. As we have also seen, a majority (but not all) carry sports, and at this point, most are found on the AM band.

What specifically is Full-Service though, and how does it differ from AC? In an essay about how fragmented radio listening became in the 80s, critic Ken Barnes described Full-Service stations as ". . . descendants of the huge MOR mainstays of the 40s, 50s and 60s; they play contemporary soft hits but place more emphasis on news, talk shows, community interaction, information, and sports. Personality counts heavily, and Full-Service is the last consistent bastion of music radio success on AM." (From Simon Frith, ed., *Facing the Music*.)

Adult Contemporary, on the other hand, tends to inhabit the FM band and is much more successful at getting the 25- to 34-year-olds than Full-Service is. AC stations are much more music-intensive, and although they may have strong service elements, music is still very important. Few ACs have a heavy sports commitment, and few have long talk blocks. Rather, the information is presented quickly and concisely so that the station's pacing never slows down too much. The music tends to be hits, but nothing with teen-appeal or with a hard-rock sound. Many ACs have a legendary morning show (such as Ron Chapman at KVIL in Dallas), and in morning drive, present as much information as one might expect from a Full-Service.

After morning drive ends though, AC stations tend to concentrate on the hits. Some even rotate their music much like a CHR (Top-40), with hits repeating every 4 to 5 hours. Depending on the type of AC, the music tends to be very familiar, with well-known artists who have current hits. It is not unusual to hear the same songs on both the CHR and the AC, although, as mentioned before, ACs will choose the softer hits, since they are striving for a slightly older audience and since they receive considerable in-office listening. ACs do play some oldies, but not as many as Full-Service stations tend to play. Full-Service stations are much more conservative musically, in most cases, because they have an older audience and want those listeners to be comfortable. Many AC stations play dance music or even Country-crossovers (songs from the Country charts that went on to become CHR hits).

In the 1960s and 70s, Adult radio was much more like MOR (although it didn't play the Frank Sinatra or Sammy Davis, Jr. songs)—it was conservative and very reticent to play any artist with a rock image. However, research showed that people who had grown up with Top-40 were *song*-oriented, not artist-oriented. That is, in the old MOR days, any song by Sinatra could be played just because Sinatra was a popular vocalist and programmers assumed the audience wanted to hear whatever songs of his were available, but after Top-40 came along, the emphasis was switched to *hit songs*: few artists, other than Elvis Presley or the Beatles, were automatically played just because of who they were. If a song didn't become a hit, Top-40s didn't keep playing it, no matter who sang it. For a long while, ACs, like MORs, added any song by so-called adult artists like Kenny Rogers, Barry Manilow, and Barbra Streisand. The new listeners coming to AC from years of Top-40 listening had no idea who Neil Diamond was, but they knew his hits because they had heard them on the Top-40s. Today, ACs do still have certain artists they are more likely to favor, but most also play whatever current Top-40 hits aren't too loud for their format. Other than music, ACs do some news and information in the afternoon (although nowhere nearly as much as a Full-Service would), and some ACs have traffic reports or their own meteorologist. Again, the main difference is that most ACs are music stations that have some information elements; most Full-Service stations are information stations that may also play some music.

In 1983, the research firm of Reymer and Gersin did a study of the various formats and who listened to them; the project, called "Radio Wars," was commissioned by the NAB and was presented at their convention that year. Even though the research was done in the early 80s, much of it still holds true. About the difference between AC and Full-Service, they wrote:

> While many Full-Service stations call themselves Adult Contemporary, Full-Service fans are radically different from A/C fans. In reality, they are a psychological "hybrid" of the News/Talk and music fans, but much more like the "News/Talkers"! The difference is mainly of *degree*. Full-Service fans seek the same intellectual stimulation that News/Talk fans do—practical information, community involvement, self-esteem, and things to think about. They just don't feel quite as strongly about these things. Like music fans, one of the main reasons they listen is for companionship . . . not a major motivation for News/Talkers. And they listen to be cheered up, while News/Talk fans don't want to be cheered up. Their ideal station would be cheerful, while News/Talk fans want a serious station . . . Full-Service fans listen for *personalities* as well as news and music. They want much more personality talk than (A/C) fans, and more entertaining "fun" talk than News/Talk fans.

Further, Reymer and Gersin divided the Full-Service listeners into four distinct groups. Using data compiled in 13 diverse markets and 1300 completed interviews, they concluded that 33% of Full-Service fans are *information junkies*, very similar to News/Talk fans, seeking lots of interesting things to think about and learn, in-depth news, and not a lot of music; 31% are *involved music fans*, who love radio, want variety, like familiar music, along with contests, features, and call-in talk shows; 26% are *cheerful sports nuts*, who don't want to learn anything in particular and mainly want entertainment and companionship, including plenty of sports, some music, and news that isn't too depressing; and finally, 10% are *habit-bound tuned-outs*, who listen very superficially, just want a quick wrap-up of news, prefer oldies, think the DJs talk too much, and like features to be brief.

Whether or not there are four types of listeners today, it is certainly true that people listen for different reasons. Full-Service listeners are not the same as CHR listeners: both groups may listen to be entertained, but clearly, a 15-year-old and a 40-year-old have different ideas about what constitutes entertainment. It is a wise manager who knows what the audience wants and expects, especially since those listeners may tune to another station if their needs are ignored.

People from urban centers like Detroit or Boston may wonder why WHO or KMA do so much farm news, but people in those markets depend on it. Similarly, while the hits are the hits everywhere, Country has yet to succeed as a format in several major eastern cities, while it is frequently number one in most southern markets. These regional differences must be taken into account when programming a station. So must *community standards*—that is, what is considered in poor taste in a certain market may seem tame elsewhere.

Many stations now do ongoing research to stay up to date on what the audience cares about and what it wants to hear about. Those stations that can't afford a big-name research firm enlist students from area colleges or design their own questionnaires and make the phone calls themselves. Designing a basic survey need not be difficult: most colleges that have business administration courses have textbooks on research methods and survey design. Also, some professors are willing to help, and their students will do the project with you in order to get hands-on experience. Not all markets have a local college, and if yours doesn't, the NAB has several useful books about how to do your own research. If you are among the fortunate stations with a sufficient budget for a nationally known research firm, you will still want to work closely with the company you choose, in order to make sure you find out exactly what you wanted to know. Some stations will find focus groups very valuable, while others will benefit more from telephone surveying. The established and experienced research firms will explain the pluses and minuses of each method so that you can decide on the right one for your station.

The point is to make sure you know what your audience thinks of your efforts. Although none of us likes criticism, it's better to find out you have a problem while you can still solve it, rather than after your audience has gone over to your competition. Some stations still distrust research or think it's a luxury, but unless you are the only station in your market, it is never a waste of time to stay on top of what the listeners are thinking. It could save you money in the long run.

The easiest research is done just by talking to local people, but surveys done at a mall or at a remote can be slanted by the fact that people might be in a hurry or they might want to give you the "right" answer since it's obvious which station you're from. Telephone surveys have the advantage of being anonymous, and thus, more objective, but be sure before you begin that you let the person on the phone know this isn't a contest and you aren't selling anything! This is a typical opening disclaimer that a telephone researcher might give before beginning a survey:

> Hello, my name is . . . and I'm from Radio Research Company. We are conducting a survey of radio listening habits in (name of city). I would like to ask you a few questions about your favorite radio station. I am not selling anything, and there are no right answers—just your opinions. The survey will only take 2 minutes. Would you be willing to participate?

If the person agrees, the surveyor will then ask some screening questions to make sure this person is appropriate for the survey. For example, if you have a Full-Service station, it wouldn't be very useful to survey 12- to 17-year-olds or 18- to 24-year-olds, as these ages don't tend to listen to the format. Also, you don't want people who never listen to radio. If possible, you want to find people who have listened to your station in the past week. However, in a market with a number of

As a group, Full-Service fans are a psychological "hybrid" of the News/Talk and music fans . . . they seek the same intellectual stimulations as News/Talk fans and the same "good feeling" from radio as music format fans. But when we take a closer look, we discover there are *four* different kinds of Full-Service fans . . . some are more like News/Talk fans while others are more like music fans . . .

The **Involved Music Fans** love *everything* about radio. They are a true Full-Service "hybrid" . . . radio cheers them up *and* makes them think.

The programming they want: Give them a multitude of features and services. Do contests, sports, and call-in shows, along with a lot of services. Musically, be traditional . . . play mainly MOR with a little contemporary.

A message that would motivate them: Tell them about your features and how they affect their lives . . . for example, "news that makes you think," or "music and personalities that cheer you up."

The **Information Junkies** are "close relatives" of News/Talk fans. They're the most serious, listening almost exclusively to think and learn.

The programming they want: Give them in-depth news reporting, and a lot of call-in talk. Also have non-news personalities who play it fairly straight. The little music you play should be mainly MOR . . . don't play much contemporary.

A message that would motivate them: Position your station as the one for "people who know what's going on."

In contrast, the **Cheerful Sports Nuts** are the most "folksy" Full-Service fans . . . they listen for sports and companionship, not to learn.

The programming they want: Be laid-back and cheerful. Play a lot of music, mixing MOR and more contemporary sounds. Have a lot of "good news" and, of course, live sports. Emphasize light topics on your talk shows. Use jingles.

A message that would motivate them: Tell them your station "keeps them company."

The **Habit-Bound Tuned-Outs** are the least involved listeners. . . they listen mainly for a quick wrap-up of the news.

The programming they want: Be traditional and predictable, but lively. Put more emphasis on contemporary "oldies" than MOR. Have short newscasts and almost no DJ talk. Have very few features, just music and news.

A message that would motivate them: They don't respond to emotional appeals, so just tell them about your programming.

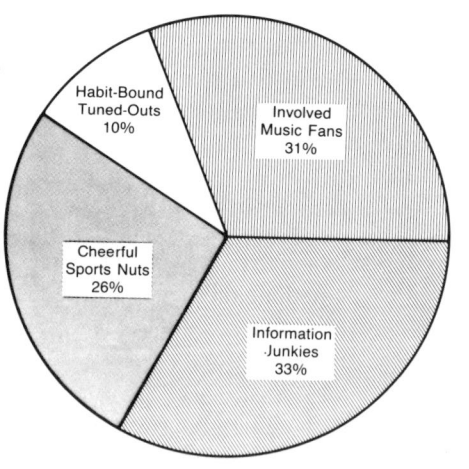

▶ *Figure 1* Full-Service Segments. *Used with permission from* Radio W. A. R. S.: How to Survive in the 80's *(National Association of Broadcasters, 1983), p.11.*

adult stations, some researchers will accept people who have listened to any Adult station or to a station that is similar to theirs. Obviously, if you are told the person only listened to Album Rock, that person wouldn't be likely to have useful data about Full-Service. With the right sample, you will get a much more accurate set of results.

Having qualified the people you want to survey, you can then administer the questionnaire itself, remembering to keep it brief and to keep it in English—not "radio-ese." Listeners don't know what a format is or what Adult Contemporary means. Phrase your questions so that people can understand them and give an honest answer. Some examples of questions you might want to ask are:

The station with the best announcers is . . . (The person responds.)
The station I listen to for news is . . .
The station where they talk too much is . . .
The station I think of as a friend is . . .
The station that has really gone downhill lately is . . .
The station I listen to the most is . . .

There are many other issues you might want to explore. Just make sure your questionnaire isn't too long, and make sure you have a clear idea of what you are trying to find out. Although some researchers may differ on what to ask, most will tell you to concentrate on actual behaviors, rather than asking someone to predict them. In other words, when you ask a listener "If a new station went on the air tomorrow, would you listen to it?", you are asking for a prediction or a guess. It's more accurate to ask questions about what the listeners are already doing, rather than what they might do in the future: "Do you listen to John Smith on WXXX?" or "I think John Smith is the best morning host . . . agree or disagree?", but *not* "If John Smith were on another station, would you listen to him?"

Research can be useful in every format, but it is especially useful in Full-Service, because so much of this format depends on being topical and knowing what matters to the audience. Full-Service listeners are very loyal to their favorite station, but first that station must win their trust.

Reymer and Gersin, in a follow-up report for the NAB in 1985 (*Radio Wars II*), observed that each format attracts a certain core group of listeners. AOR and CHR, for example, attract large numbers of *social followers*, a predominantly young group of people who listen to radio frequently and use their favorite station as a social experience—something they can do with their friends. They like current music, enjoy contests, and find news both uninteresting and depressing. They look to their favorite station to energize them, and they prefer a lively, cheerful station.

Contrast that group with the majority of Full-Service listeners, whom Reymer and Gersin label *friend seekers*. This group is mostly over 35 years old, white, and white-collar. They like news, as well as intellectual stimulation. They don't mind music, but they want a good mix of music and information. They like air personalities who are interesting and entertaining, and the main reason they listen is for companionship when they are lonely. For these people, Full-Service radio keeps them company as well as keeping them informed.

64   Full-Service Radio

Like News/Talk fans, Full-Service fans even regard their favorite station as a way to learn those interesting things that will enhance their stature with other people. They see themselves as more discerning and more aware than those who don't listen. Knowing this, some stations have used positioning slogans like "WXXX,Where You Learn Something New Every Day." Few listeners want an educational station, that is, one that is pedantic or talks down to them, but the idea of learning something or becoming more knowledgeable appeals to most Full-Service listeners, especially if it is accomplished in a friendly, personable context.

Although Full-Service fans like the service elements of the format, they definitely don't want the station to have an overly serious manner. They like to enjoy good conversation, hear from an interesting guest, and learn both sides of an issue, but they don't want to feel as if they are being lectured. Good Full-Service stations know that if the listeners feel overwhelmed or patronized, they will leave.

So how is Full-Service different today from, let's say, a decade ago? What does today's audience expect? The consensus of many experienced Full-Service program

	Old America	*New America*
Radio Environment		
Number of radio stations	6180 (1978)	9003 (1988)
Number of FM radio stations	1944 (1978)	4089 (1988)
Radio ad revenue (millions)	$3052 (1978)	$7745 (1988)
FM share of tuning	46% (Fall 1978)	76% (Fall 1988)
Technology	Audio landlines	Satellite delivery
	Mimeograph courier	Fax
	Turntable	CD player
	Transistor	Microchip
	Electric typewriter	Word processor/PC
	Large, component stereo	Portable stereo
	Boom box	Walkman
	Color TV	VCR/stereo TV
	Network TV dominates	Cable TV grows
	AT&T phones	"Smart" phones
	Operator Answering service	Portable answering service
	Pocket calculators	Laptop computers
	Records	Cassettes/CDs
	Broadcast radio	More "cable radio"
Television		
Channel penetration	31% receive more than 8 TV channels	85% receive more than 8 TV channels
	3 networks	Pay/cable channels

▶ *Figure 2   Old America–New America Comparison Chart. Used with permission from Programming Radio to Win in the New America (National Association of Broadcasters, 1989), p. 5.*

directors is that the biggest change in the past 10 years has been the increased number of choices. In 1989, the NAB presented a study done by John Parikhal and David Oakes of Joint Communications in Toronto. The study, *Programming to Win in the New America,* discussed the ways in which radio listening had changed from 1978 to 1988. All major formats were looked at, and nearly 500 program directors were surveyed so that they could express their opinions and concerns. Some of the changes that Parikhal and Oakes discussed in their report included:

1. The 25- to 54-year-old age group continued to increase. As the baby boomers aged, by 1988 42% of the U.S. population was between the ages of 25 and 54.
2. The work week increased. Where in 1978 workers expected more time off, by 1988 many people found themselves working longer hours. Along with this, in 1978, workers expected their income would grow, whereas in 1988 the perception of the average person was that it was more difficult to make ends meet, and annual family income was not keeping up with inflation.
3. By 1988, there were more women in the work force, more two-income marriages, and more divorces and step-families than in 1978. Also, the United States birth rate continued to decline.

Figure 2 (Continued)

		Old America	New America
Financial			
Radio Station Resale Values			
(Examples)			
KMEO-AM/FM	Phoenix	$4,000,000 (1980)	$16,000,000 (1985)
KJOI-FM	Los Angeles	$18,500,000 (1984)	$44,000,000 (1985)
KFAC-AM/FM	Los Angeles	$7,700,000 (1970)	$33,500,000 (1986)
KAHI -AM/			
KHYL-FM	Sacramento	$25,000 (1977)	$8,000,000 (1986)
WLVH-FM	Hartford	$160,000 (1969)	$4,500,000 (1986)

Lifestyle	1978	1988
	37 % of population is 25-54.	42% of population is 25-54.
	Workers anticipate decrease in work week.	Work week increases 20% vs. 1978.
	People anticipate increase in leisure time.	Leisure time decreases by 30% vs. 1978.
	People anticipate big "real" increase in family income	Annual family income increases only $828 in 10 years (well below inflation).

The New America features more choices and less time to make those choices. The environment in which today's radio programmer must work is cluttered more than ever with messages and technology.

Competition now features not only station against station but radio against all other media.

4. The new technology affected more people. By 1988 fax machines, videocassette recorders (VCRs), personal computers, and CD players were very popular. Also, over 60% of cars had cassette players in addition to the AM/FM radio. On the TV side, where in 1978 the networks dominated, by 1988, cable-TV had achieved considerable acceptance in most cities.
5. In 1978, there were 6180 radio stations. By 1988, there were 9003. Of these, in 1978, 1944 were FM, where by 1988, it had grown to 4089, and, where 46% of listeners tuned to FM in 1978, by 1988 it was 76%.

A number of books were written during the 80s about the way American society had become busier, more pressured, with less leisure time. In the frequently quoted book by Ries and Trout, *Positioning, The Battle For Your Mind,* the authors talked at length about the problems inherent in an overcommunicated society like ours. They noted, for example, that with only 6% of the world's population, Americans consume 57% of the world's advertising. Each year, some 30,000 books are published. American newspapers use more than ten million tons of newsprint. Ninety-eight percent of all Americans own at least one TV set. The average American family watches 51 hours of TV a week. Americans are constantly being barraged with information to process, to such a great degree that some people feel overloaded. Companies with huge advertising budgets promote their products on radio and TV, on billboards, in magazines, and on designer-label clothing. There are more brands than ever, and many people have a difficult time distinguishing between them all. How is a Chevrolet different from a Ford? How is one shampoo different from another? In radio, how are a number of stations that are all playing basically the same music and all trying to reach the 25- to 54-year-old adult able to stand out in the listener's mind?

For Ries and Trout, the answer comes from *positioning.* To succeed in our overcommunicated society, with all those messages and all those choices, a product (or, in this case, a radio station) must have its own position. Since perception is reality, what people believe about a product is the truth for them, no matter what the facts might dictate. Thus, if your station is perceived as the station with the most reliable news, no matter what clever slogans your competition might try, you own that position, and they don't. This works negatively too: if you are perceived as the station that has too much talk or too many commercials, that's the position you own, and it's up to you to create a new and more favorable impression.

Usually, Ries and Trout tell us, it's best to be the *first* to do something. Hertz and IBM are two examples of companies perceived as having gotten there first, and once people believe a good product was originated by a certain company, they are likely to think of that company rather than any of its competitors. The key is *top-of-the-mind awareness.* In your market, which station comes to mind first, and why? The heritage Full-Service stations like KDKA and KMOX have done an excellent job at this.

In fact, many Full-Service stations encourage this perception with positioning statements that stress their involvement with their local area. WTSO in Madison, Wisconsin, has used the slogan "WTSO . . . we're all about Dane County"; they further localized this by putting up billboards in specific towns, and each billboard named that town instead of Dane County. This technique reinforced the perception that while WTSO covered the entire county, it also paid attention to all the cities and towns within the county. WHO has used "Des Moines' News Station" very successfully. Some stations want people to closely associate their call letters with the city itself, such as "WJR Stands For Detroit." A number of Full-Service stations use slogans based on their image as dependable or reliable: both WSB and WMAL have used "Depend On It," while WHAS told listeners to "Depend On Us." KSL in Salt Lake City has used both "The News Authority" and "When You Want To Know First, Come To KSL." Numerous Full-Service stations, WGY among them, have used "information" in their positioning statements, as in, "Your Information Station."

The reason for all this is to increase listener awareness. Since both Birch and Arbitron ask people to recall what stations they have been listening to, the only way to get good ratings is to make sure people remember your station. If they don't, they might give credit to some other station, even if they were really listening to yours. That is why slogans and statements have become important. Some new announcers might find it boring to read them verbatim from a card, but their purpose is to remind the listeners of the station's benefits.

Ries and Trout also explained the importance of finding the right niche, finding a particular need the audience has, and doing an excellent job of dealing with it. Stations like WHO and WBZ became known as the most complete resources for school closings and cancellations during bad weather. Other stations became known for carrying the most important sports events, having a particularly controversial talk host, providing the most accurate weather, or providing a consistently entertaining morning show.

Some All News stations, observing the changes in the lifestyles of their audience, took the position of giving people the news *fast* as well as first: "Give us twenty-two minutes and we'll give you the world" (a slogan which basically admits that the top stories, like hit songs, will be repeated so that people who just tuned in won't have to wait a long time to hear them). This position worked well for the Cable News Network (CNN); it offered a full hour-long newscast with more in-depth stories, but it also offered an offshoot called "Headline News" which gave news, sports, celebrity updates and consumer information in a fast-paced half-hour format. In some markets, people are very rushed and they appreciate news that is thorough but brief.

If you know your audience, you can adjust your station's style accordingly and be more in-depth at some times and more fast-paced at others, but however your station decides to present its service elements, it is important to make sure the listeners feel they are getting what they want. In our overcommunicated society, people no longer believe (or remember) all the vague claims they hear—hundreds of products say they are "the best," "new," "improved," or "better." Because of fragmentation, stations today tend to be much more specific when promoting themselves so that the audience will be very sure where to turn for news or information or oldies or whatever.

Russ Wood, the general manager of KSL, explains the strategy that led the station to gradually eliminate music and highlight talk and features. "We realized that even though we were technically advanced and our engineers had provided the audience with excellent audio quality, we still couldn't compete with the FM music stations. But our research told us we owned the news image in Salt Lake City. So we decided to expand on that."

This attitude is echoed by many managers of successful Full-Service stations. Chuck Jewell of WHO says, "We never let ourselves get caught up in trying to compete with the FMs. They have their strengths, but we have ours, and we concentrate on those strengths, like our news, sports, and farm coverage."

Roy Cooper of WIBC in Indianapolis adds, "We've never paid attention to the so-called decline of AM. We've carved out our own niche. When we say we are the 'Voice of News for Indiana,' the listeners know we mean it. Having 50,000 watts is certainly an advantage, but that's not what makes a station successful: it's how you cover your market."

Jimmy Barrett of WJR says, "The main reason AM radio is in danger of dying is the defeatist attitude of some AM stations. If your station provides what people need, if it offers interesting program choices, if it promotes itself, the fact that it's on AM doesn't have to be a problem."

According to Ries and Trout, the best way to find the right position for your station is to ask yourself some questions about how the audience currently perceives what you are doing:

1. What position do you own?
2. What position would you like to own?
3. Whom must you outgun to get that position?
4. Do you have enough money to attain the position you want?
5. Do you have the time and patience to hang in there?
6. Do you put forth the right image for the position you want?

To explain in a little more detail, since perception is reality, the audience may see you far differently from how you want to be seen. As a consultant, I've watched stations change format and discover later on that the audience still thought of them as what they used to be. So, first, look honestly at what people think you are. In their minds, are you the station for old people? The news authority? The teen rock station? Once you've learned what the average person thinks your station is, consider whether or not that's the message you've tried to convey. Many good products over the years have been hurt by inaccurate or erroneous beliefs people had about them. If you've tried to market your station as one thing but the audience thinks you're something entirely different, there's a failure to communicate somewhere.

Getting angry at the audience for not having the right opinion won't solve the problem. Analyze what sort of promotion you've done. If you spent money on billboards, what was on those billboards? Were they too hard to read? Were they impossible to see from a distance? Did they fail to convey something positive about your station? In an effort to save some money, did you have half a billboard for your AM and half for your FM, with two contradictory and potentially confusing messages? Maybe billboards aren't effective in your market and it's time for some other method. The point is, just because something sounded good or worked well in 1975 doesn't mean it still does in the 1990s. Stations that rest on their past successes seldom get any new ones.

So study the market carefully, and plan how you intend to guide the audience to think of you the way you want them to. Who currently occupies the position you want—another station, the local newspaper, or maybe cable news? Whoever occupies it now, that doesn't mean they always will. People's needs change, as do their lifestyles. What an 18-year-old wants from radio is usually entertainment; what a 45-year-old wants may include information.

If you used to be number one, that is a position you may be able to regain, although probably not with the same techniques you used 20 years ago. Are you really committed to working your way back to the top? Some stations want quick fixes and magic answers.

Unfortunately, in today's competitive marketplace, there are few easy solutions to complicated problems. Winning the audience back after you've lost them or attracting a new audience to replace the older end of your demographics are not 3-month propositions. Even CHR (Top-40) stations that used to give away huge sums of cash during a rating period are finding that their competition is doing the same thing. Money alone won't get you a loyal audience. What money will do is enable you to improve your image, make your station more visible (another news car, a van with your call letters on it), and possibly enable you to hire more experienced staff.

Today, many stations are being sold for incredible sums, and the new owners need a fast return on their investment. Building a winning station, especially in a format like Full-Service, takes time. Yes, Full-Service does tend to have very high cume (large numbers of people who tune in to sample the station), so you will probably be able to persuade people to try you again even if they didn't like your station before. What will make them stay, however, is consistent, interesting programming, and that doesn't just happen. It requires a serious commitment.

Even in small markets, because there are more choices, stations can no longer risk giving the audience bad radio. It may be unrealistic for a small station to sound like one in a major market, but it is not unrealistic to expect even a small station to display professionalism. When announcers go out to do remotes, how do they dress? What does your equipment look like? Granted, a small-market station may not have thousands of dollars for state-of-the-art gadgets, but if you do your remotes on a rickety card table with lots of tangled wires and a hand-painted sign, you are making a statement about your station. Sometimes, it is the little things that mean a lot. When people from the community come to your station, what do they see? Do you display the awards you've won? Is your reception area clean and pleasant-looking? You may wonder what that has to do with getting listeners, but even in the large markets, Full-Service stations are thought of as a friend, and you will gain plenty of goodwill by having a station environment that local people, both clients and listeners, can feel comfortable visiting.

This also applies to your image in the community—do you strive to make people feel good about your station? Do you answer your mail? When someone calls with a complaint, what is the procedure? You don't have to change your programming to suit every listener who calls; all most people want is to be taken seriously. Nothing upsets a listener more than expressing an opinion and having the station ignore it. At least have the courtesy to reply, even if your reply is an explanation of why that talk show they hate is going to remain on the air. Some stations have allowed themselves to be perceived as arrogant and inapproachable by seeming to have contempt for the audience. As any good account executive knows, a customer should not be treated as a bother, and, as any good programmer also knows, a station that treats its listeners well will benefit from doing so.

When you read the fan letters people write to their favorite stations, you can see tangible proof of this. WJR has received hundreds of letters of thanks as a result of its "Call for Action" program, during which trained volunteers help listeners resolve a wide range of problems, from consumer issues to landlord-tenant disputes to bureaucratic runarounds. One typical thank-you letter to WJR said in part, "After dealing with XXX company for over six months and getting nowhere, you took my problem and resolved it in two weeks! Many thanks to all of you for the wonderful work you are doing." On a more personal matter, WMT regularly receives letters like this: "Thank you so much for the dozen roses I received for my 79th birthday. I shared them with my husband, who is in a nursing home. They are the center of attraction in the main lounge and are still beautiful after five days. Thank you again!" Stations like WJR and WMT are among those that recognize the value of making the listener feel important. It's a strategy that, if done with sincerity, can help your station build and keep a positive reputation.

To sum up, the research of Parikhal and Oakes points out that programming a successful Adult radio station today is more challenging than ever. Ninety percent of all the AC and Full-Service program directors they interviewed said that the number one problem their stations face is that listeners feel too many stations sound the same. Further, these program directors feel that as a result of too many media choices, listener loyalty has declined, and it is more difficult to make listeners aware of what makes a particular station special. Many program directors are using direct mail as a way to put their station's call letters in people's homes. Others prefer focus groups. (Focus groups are popular with both News/Talk and Full-Service stations because in a focus group, there is in-depth discussion and the opportunity to get much more specific feedback than could be obtained from a brief telephone survey.)

All the program directors agreed, however, that their situation was not impossible, that loyalty *can* be built, through having interesting personalities and very localized information, as well as doing a thorough job of promoting the station. As long as Full-Service stations continue to concentrate on *service* in a way that many other formats don't, people will turn to them. As for how to give these listeners something worth turning to, some suggestions follow in the next two chapters.

8
How To Do Full-Service: The Right Programming

Full-Service AM stations began the 1990s with some problems that still remained unsolved. One was the confusion over AM-stereo. A number of state-of-the-art AMs immediately adopted this new technology as soon as it became available. Unfortunately, confusion resulted when no official standard was agreed upon, and AM-stereo receivers were never marketed with any consistency. Some car manufacturers did provide automobiles that had AM-stereo, but again, no consistent marketing plan really emphasized this to anyone.

Meanwhile, in several surveys done by reputable research firms, it was found that large numbers of people believed they were listening to AM-stereo even though they weren't. Yet, more than half of the people one researcher interviewed said that stereo greatly improved AM, while at the same time saying that just because an AM station was stereo this wouldn't make them listen to it more!

On the other hand, since the rise of FM, most listeners have accepted the fact that FMs sound cleaner than and have superior audio quality to AMs. In a 1987 NAB survey, 60% of those surveyed mentioned some type of interference during AM listening. Also, dissatisfaction was expressed with the audio quality currently found on AM (the standard currently in use had not been upgraded since the FCC adopted it in 1946). A new standard was finally agreed upon in 1990, but it was not yet fully in place as this book went to press. Meanwhile, some stations waited patiently for the FCC to clear up the confusion, while others just went on doing the best they could with what they had.

Another problem for AM Full-Service in the new decade was financial. Ad revenues throughout the 80s increased on FM, and so did listenership. AM found itself saddled with the image of a medium whose audience was slowly dying off. The researchers emerged again and found that the main reasons given for preferring FM were that AM played too many commercials, AM had poor sound quality, and young people had become accustomed to hearing their favorite music on FM.

But the story wasn't completely tragic. AM had strong listenership in morning drive (and, interestingly, during the overnights, especially in markets where most stations signed off before midnight, and those AM clear channel powerhouses remained on the air all night). It also had strong specialty listening, such as listening for big sports events or for in-depth news reporting. In farm-oriented areas, AM was

▼ 72   Full-Service Radio

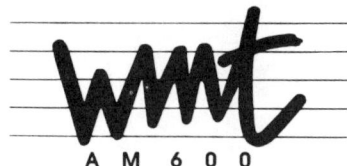

PROGRAMMING

A Statement of Philosophy

WMT is THE radio station for thousands of midwesterners whose tastes demand responsible, informative radio programming. News responsibilities are met by nearly round-the-clock radio news personnel. Eastern Iowans have come to trust the reporting of News Director Don Wilson and the WMT News team. Our local news involvement is coupled with national coverage by CBS Radio, long recognized as the "Number One radio network for news and sports." Speaking of sports, WMT originates its own coverage of all the University of Iowa's major sporting programs. Sports Director Ron Gonder and Sports Editor Kevin Dolan bring you up-to-the-minute sports reports beginning at 6:09 a.m. Daily reports run throughout the broadcast day, seven days a week. City and country dwellers alike have long received their weather information from WMT, staffed by full-time, accredited meteorologist Greg Story. Our heavy involvement in agribusiness is obvious; WMT is one of very few stations to have two full-time farm broadcasters, Farm Director Jerry Passer and Farm Editor Rich Balvanz.

And entertainment? That's handled by a dedicated, experienced staff of adult personalities who are encouraged to use their minds as well as their mouths. Jerry Carr, Steve Carpenter, Gary Edwards, and Bob Carpenter are creative and audience-involving, providing quality, yet fun programs that listeners expect. Additional specialty programs are handled by Leo Greco, Jim Doyne, Andy Scott, and Jim Dalton. WMT has evolved musically, resulting in a tasteful blend of today's adult music selections, "crossover" country hits, and an intermixing of pop album standards.

Reliable information and quality entertainment are the reasons WMT is ranked among the top radio stations in the United States. Audiences and advertisers continue to look to WMT for responsive programming to meet the needs of informed and entertained adults throughout WMT's 5-state service area.

P.O. BOX 2147 • 600 OLD MARION ROAD N.E. • CEDAR RAPIDS, IOWA 52406 • 319-395-0530

▶ *Figure 3   A page from WMT's media kit. Most successful Full-Service stations have professionally-printed packages of material about their achievements and benefits. These kits are given to potential advertisers and community leaders to make them more familiar with what the station offers.*
Courtesy WMT, Cedar Rapids.

also counted on. In very small towns with not many stations around for miles, it didn't matter if the station were AM or FM—it was the community station, and people listened to it.

Still, it cannot be denied that many AMs lost money during the 80s, especially daytimers and stand-alones (those without an FM sister station). Some owners who tried to sell their AMs found that their value had depreciated, while FMs in general appreciated. News/Talk, Full-Service, and Country were the most successful AM formats in the 80s, although ethnic stations (Black, Hispanic) did well in some markets as did some religious stations. Overall, the average full-time AM lost about $4000 during 1988, according to NAB research; the average daytimer lost more than $13,000.

Once again, however, certain AM stations overcame the predictions of doom and continued to make a sizeable profit, in addition to maintaining solid ratings. The fact that the population was aging did not prove to be a negative either. Another interesting lifestyle change of the 80s was a new respect for people in their fifties and sixties. TV shows started featuring older people as characters. Several of these shows earned huge ratings. Also, older people were being portrayed more in commercials, and products were being marketed to them. Despite American culture still being youth-oriented, demographers were observing that the 50-year-old and older audience was healthy and had money to spend.

Writing in *American Demographics* magazine (which, by the way, no successful sales or programming manager should be without) in June of 1989, James Golub and Harold Javitz noted the same phenomenon about older Americans that researchers Reymer and Gersin had seen in radio listeners: instead of stereo-typing 50-five-year-old and over adults as a monolithic group, Golub and Javitz found six distinct groups, each differing in their attitudes about life. Among them were *explorers*, who are self-reliant individualists who want to do things their way, are in good health, well-educated, and enjoy both cultural and recreational activities; *adapters*, who are very extroverted, value their friends and their possessions, enjoy leisure activities such as golf or swimming, and don't mind spending money for entertainment; and on the other extreme are *martyrs*, who dislike change, are very introverted, don't have a lot of money to spend, feel that medical care is very important, tend to live with their children or with relatives, and see religion as a central part of their life.

The point of such research is to make business people more aware of what 55-year-old and over adults expect today so that they can market their product or service effectively. With large groups of older adults enjoying their retirement yet still keeping up with news and information, radio stations in areas with a large 55-year-old and over population can reach out to them in a way that makes a impact.

There is still a generation gap at some of the advertising agencies, however: buyers tend to be young, and some still maintain the stereotypic belief that all 55-year-old and over adults are martyrs when in reality, the majority display few of those traits. Stations with audiences that are largely over 50 are having to do some consciousness-raising at some of the agencies to demonstrate that older Americans are a viable force with free time and disposable income. Having what some call an "older audience" need not be considered a liability.

What do we know about AM listeners in general? Several studies were done in the 80s, and according to this research, a typical AM listener tends to have a slightly higher income; is a day person rather than a night person; feels greater ties to the past; is generally satisfied with life; isn't very interested in current music trends but likes the music he or she grew up with; and is easier to entertain musically, but very particular about information, news, and features. Also, the AM listener is less likely to change jobs or move within the next 5 years and prefers watching sports to participating in them. AM listeners read the newspaper more than FM listeners, and they watch more TV.

All this is especially useful to know because as the baby boomers continue to age, whatever demographic they are in will be very influential, just because of the sheer numbers. When they were in the 12- to 17-year-old age group, they certainly made their presence felt, and since the late 50s, advertisers have made reaching them a priority. That in itself explains the sudden emergence during the late 70s and early 80s of a variety of formats aimed at 25- to 44-year-old adults. With the baby boomers approaching the 45- to 54-year-old age group, it will be interesting to see how both programmers and advertisers respond and what style of radio the baby boomers will want.

The older baby boomers (those born in the late 40s) grew up with Top-40, while the younger boomers grew up with AM already declining and FM winning the young audience. For that reason, AM Oldies stations have managed to survive nicely, given that AM fans are also fans of the music they were raised with, namely rock hits from the 50s and 60s.

Will these older oldies still be relevant to the 50-year-old baby boomer? Some Full-Service stations, WGY and WLW among them, have decided that they are better off to play more 70s oldies, in an effort to bring in the 35-year-old boomers, and cut back on the really old oldies (except perhaps on a special "Million Dollar Weekend"). Obviously, those stations that have eliminated most music (KSL, WHO, KMOX, and others), don't have to worry about what oldies from what years are advantageous, but some Full-Service stations still believe that music is a service, and they have no plans to drop it in the immediate future.

Numerous respected consultants, including Rick Sklar (who used to program the most successful AM Top-40 in the East, WABC) have predicted that it won't be long before AM will be all talk and information. New advances in technology may keep that from happening; also, in some markets, especially those community stations with no real competition, people may accept music on AM with no question, since there is no other alternative in their area. Unique formats have succeeded this way: in my own travels, I've seen AM hard-rock stations win a large number of young people in a market where nobody on FM was playing anything for 12- to 24-year olds. The same holds true for AM Urban/Black stations in areas where nobody else is serving them.

It may not be a popular move to play a lot of music on AM, in a time when AM supposedly owns older people and news fans only, but again, every market is special in some way, and an interesting AM that has music a large number of people want but can't get may very well carve out a niche for itself. As many FM stations abandon Beautiful Music because it allegedly appeals only to the oldest demographics, it will be interesting to see if any AM stations try it out.

What then, makes a Full-Service station successful? Must you have legendary call letters like KDKA or WBZ? Do you need 50,000 watts like WSB or WCCO? Is there a list of do's and don't's that these stations use? As we discussed in Chapter 6, many Full-Service stations have adapted to changes in the audience. Some markets are very transient—Washington D.C., for example, has many military and government personnel moving in and out. While there are certainly long-term D.C.-area residents, new people relocating into WMAL's signal range every year give the station a great opportunity to attract more listeners; at the same time, WMAL is also able to reinforce its value for its established audience. Since WMAL is aware of the fluctuations in its market, it knows that constant promotion is necessary so that the WMAL call letters and image will always be in front of as many people as possible.

Like the greater D.C. area, other markets have their own individual characteristics, which are useful for stations to keep in mind. Some have extremes of weather, such as hurricanes or tornadoes. Some have massive influxes of visitors during the winter months (such as parts of Texas where many retirees, called "Winter Texans" vacation). Some have a local economy that depends on tourism (such as Las Vegas or Orlando). Some markets change during the ski season or the fishing season. Some change when a major new attraction, such as an amusement park or a giant shopping mall, is built there. Some change because of a decline in business, caused by plant closings or the town's leading industry falling on hard times (such as what happened in parts of Michigan when the auto makers suffered losses and laid off workers).

Few markets today are identical to how they were 20 years ago, and it's a mistake to run a station as if nothing has ever changed. Some managers who have lived in a town all their life find it difficult to be objective about how their station really sounds, especially when clients and friends (who have also always lived there) say it sounds fine to them. It never hurts to get an outside opinion, which is why even in smaller markets, some managers bring in a consultant several times a year just to make sure the station is keeping up with today's audience.

Also, few stations do only one big promotion anymore, even in markets that are only rated once a year. Visibility is crucial in today's competitive radio arena. Even those stations which have a limited promotion budget can still promote by being seen at the important town meetings, interviewing the major newsmakers, and having vehicles and microphone shields that display the station call letters prominently. Since perception is reality, creating the perception that your station is *everywhere* will keep people thinking about it and help give it top-of-the-mind awareness.

The one rule that any successful station, whether big-signal major market or small-market community-oriented, must remember is *know your audience*. Many stations waste a lot of time and money because they make assumptions about the listeners. Part of the problem is that, especially in those smaller markets, the announcers are just starting out and may be much younger than the target audience. They often have no idea how to do Adult radio, having come from college stations that did CHR or AOR.

Fortunately, there are some definite steps even an inexperienced staff can take to become more familiar with the concerns and interests of the audience. Consultant Jay Mitchell suggests that the program director train young announcers to be more aware of their community. This is done by making them responsible for finding out about such local events as births and marriages, who got promoted at work, who got elected to a local office, or who was appointed to chair a service organization. The sources for this information would include the local newspaper, press releases, public-service announcements sent to the station, and the publicity directors at the various organizations such as Lions Club, Rotary, Kiwanis, Shriners, church and synagogue social action groups, and any important local charitable organizations. Although a young DJ might not think being honored at a Rotary meeting is a big deal, to the person receiving the honor, it's very special, as it is to that person's friends who may hear about it for the first time when the station sends out congratulations over the air.

Mitchell also suggests that these local facts be put on file cards, with a kill date on them, as would be done with a public-service announcement. They can then be rotated throughout the air shifts and changed every few days to keep them fresh and up to date; doing this creates the perception that the listeners are part of an extended family, and the station enjoys being able to salute "family members." Including the achievements of the local Merchants Association and the Chamber of Commerce is also a good idea. Stations like WMT and KMA have earned considerable goodwill in the community from their eagerness to praise local products and events. It takes time and effort to build a credible community presence, but the rewards are well worth it.

Why do some stations seem to resist being "more local"? Although generalities are seldom useful, it does seem to be true in many smaller markets that the announcers and the program director (PD) are relatively new and plan to be in that market for as short a time as possible before moving up to someplace bigger. A town that is just a stepping-stone for a young announcer may be very special to a lifelong resident, who is proud of the area and has no desire to leave. This difference in goals can affect how a station is programmed.

Full-Service is not a format that can be learned in 10 minutes nor is it as simple as "shut up and play the hits." On the other hand, it is a format that inspires great devotion and loyalty from the audience if it is done well. Some PDs, in their well-meaning attempt to be sophisticated, assume that local mentions are passé, but to the resident of the market, hearing good news about something a neighbor achieved is interesting. What we may feel is old-fashioned or corny, the audience may associate with friendship and sociability. That in itself is all the more reason why becoming familiar with the audience is essential for a winning station.

What about promotion? Not all stations have $50,000 to give away nor can they come up with diamonds or trips to Europe, but maybe that's not what every listener really wants. Some researchers have found that trips are seen as more trouble than they're worth: the winner has to get time off from work, find a baby-sitter for the kids, make arrangements for carpools to be covered, etc. Some people would very much enjoy Paris in the springtime, but more of them would enjoy having their bills paid. Even though the 1980s saw the emergence of the *yuppie* and the *buppie* and the *dink* (young, upwardly mobile urban professional, black upwardly mobile urban professional, and double-income household with no kids), most people felt that their income no longer stretched as far as it used to, and middle-class people especially felt inflation was taking a large chunk out of their paycheck.

When asked by researchers what prize they really wanted, some people said a new car or a vacation, but the majority said money. Perhaps in New York City, that means enormous sums, but in most markets, a $50 bill can generate lots of excitement, as can tickets to a major sporting event or a free dinner at a nice restaurant. Bigger isn't always better. We've all heard people win a big prize and sound totally unenthusiastic, while a listener who won a comparatively small prize playing "trivia" couldn't have been happier.

Successful Full-Service stations offer prizes that will in some way make the listener's life easier. WTIC, which has the resources to do so, has given away a house. Other smaller stations have paid the winner's rent or mortgage, or given them a day off with pay. Some stations create a special evening, with a limousine ride to a nice restaurant, a romantic dinner, and tickets to a play. Some give away CD players or VCRs, or whatever the hot new item with the latest technology is (in the late 80s, it was personal fax machines or lap-top computers). A week's worth of groceries is always appreciated. So is a shopping spree at a clothing store.

Whatever prizes you offer, make sure they are things the listeners would want to have, rather than just whatever the sales department was able to trade out that week. Try in some way to make listeners' wishes and dreams come true, such as reuniting family members who haven't seen each other in years, or sending some kids whose parents couldn't afford it to summer camp. Even if you can't do what KVIL in Dallas did in 1985 when it gave away a new car every week for ten weeks, you can still give the audience something enjoyable, especially if the contest is fun to listen to. Most people don't believe they'll ever win, and many won't even call, so any contests you run should be entertaining even for the people who don't intend to participate.

As many stations no longer just do one big promotion a year, they also avoid just having one big prize. Unless the big prize is so amazing that thousands of people would fight over it, having one big prize usually creates resentment among all the people who won nothing. Stations are better off having a number of good prizes to offset the one great prize. That way, a lot of listeners will be happy instead of only one. Also, if bigger isn't necessarily better, more isn't always better. Don't have too many contests going on simultaneously: it just makes you sound as if you're trying to bribe the audience. Contests that are challenging yet winnable can be just one more good reason to listen to your station.

Now, the news. If there is one element that has become almost synonymous with Full-Service radio, it's information. Although the need for information hasn't changed over the years, the way in which today's stations present it has changed greatly. As you know, in radio's early days, announcers were expected to educate; they spoke with perfect diction and were supposed to set an example for how the English language should be used. That overly serious style was also a part of newsreading. Critics in popular magazines of the day spoke out against using any slang or collo-quial speech. Since many of the larger stations were owned by a newspaper, and since news departments were a later development, stations like WGN derived their news reports from the newspaper (in their case, the *Chicago Tribune*), and read them verbatim. The networks may have had a few well-known journalists, but at the local level, news reporting was slow to emerge as a priority. Once stations realized how much people really did want news, they began providing it, but the same formal style prevailed.

When Top-40 came along, media watchers were interested to see how news would be handled: it was still an FCC requirement that news be aired, yet Top-40 was supposed to be a format aimed at teenagers, few of whom seemed concerned with serious matters. Top-40 stations did do the news—except they shortened the length of the casts and gave it catchy names like "Twenty/Twenty News" (it was on at twenty past or twenty of the hour, rather than the traditional top-of-the-hour position).

At the time, I'm sure not many people considered the significance of how Top-40 did the news. Years later, however, this very minor element to the Top-40 audience would become a more important part of AC radio. The young adults entering into the 25- to 34-year-old demographic were coming to AC with far different expectations than those 45-year-old and over adults who had never grown up with Top-40. As they outgrew teen music, as their lives changed, as they married or began careers or had kids, 24- to 34-year-old adults turned to a more adult form of entertainment. Unlike older adults who could still recall the Golden Age of Radio, these baby boomers had grown up with TV, in addition to Top-40. They had a much shorter attention span, didn't read as much, and while they wanted to know what was going on, they didn't expect an in-depth 10-minute news report read by someone in a very serious voice. Those adults who had been raised on Top-40 wanted AC to reflect their fast-paced lives, as well as the right-to-the-point news they had heard on Top-40.

Meanwhile, TV was going through its own evolution, from the early days of serious male journalists with reputations for thorough reporting, to the much-maligned days of "happy talk" where anchors hired mainly for their good looks smiled and joked with each other in an effort to make the news more friendly, to a more moderate approach where men and women who were both attractive and good reporters did serious stories along with human interest pieces.

The late 80s brought a form of journalism derisively called *Tabloid TV* which featured stories that were often shocking or controversial, about subjects previously not considered news (exposés on the more unusual sexual practices of certain celebrities, profiles of people who had committed especially degrading crimes, etc.). Although the critics were appalled, some of these shows got very strong ratings, and led some traditional TV stations to start seeking out blood, gore, and guts stories during their prime-time casts.

Part of the way TV news changed allowed the emergence of CNN, a network devoted exclusively to the old-fashioned in-depth news reporting radio and TV had once done. CNN reporters spoke naturally, but they were not hired for their looks: some were in fact attractive, but all were respected professionals for whom covering the news accurately and completely was of major importance. While local TV stations looked for gimmicks to raise ratings and revenues, and while many stations shortened their news broadcasts or did a greater number of stories superficially, those who wanted a lot of news could go over to cable and get it there, 24 hours a day.

As for radio, more women began doing the news in the 80s (previously sexist thinking prevented them from doing so—the stereotypic excuse I heard during the 60s and early 70s was that women didn't have the voice for serious news, and when a woman read the news, it would sound like gossip), and some of the other changes were similar to those of TV.

As TV news viewers split into two distinct groups, one of which wanted the traditional style and the other of which wanted news delivered in English the average person could understand, radio news had similar problems. One group expected long newscasts with lots of detail and an announcing style called "voice of doom" by its detractors. The other, younger group preferred less detail, and a much more conversational, even idiomatic style. The older group regarded this as heresy: having become accustomed to news the way the newspapers wrote it (that newspaper influence was still felt in the way the wire services and certain news reporters presented the news), they found this new way of doing it far too superficial. For these people, Full-Service and News/Talk were godsends, since both formats still offered much more than just a couple of quick sentences and a sound bite. Even here, however, the baby boomers would have some effect.

As many news reporters and writers went to work at Full-Service stations, they brought with them the radio they knew best—and for a lot of them, it had been Top-40 or AOR. Since not everyone working in Full-Service was in the 50-year-old and over demographic, this influx of new ideas from experienced but young (25- to 34-year-old) journalists, plus the awareness of the shorter attention span of today's adults, led even traditional Full-Service and MOR stations to do some modernizing. This was especially necessary if Full-Service wanted to attract any of that under 30-year-old audience to AM. Some tuned in for sports or for storm cancellations. The theory was that if news could be written in a more interesting and dynamic manner, these adults might feel more comfortable listening, and they might stay with the station longer.

Today, most Full-Service stations still try to offer some in-depth coverage, some investigative journalism, some human interest, and some amusing pieces, but they are written and delivered as if speaking to a friend. Smaller stations which lack a large news staff may still rely on the wire services, but even there, newsreaders are editing the wire copy to make it easier to understand, and eliminating phrases that sound like journalese. This more relaxed (yet still accurate) style has also found its way into public-service announcements, where clichés like "the public is invited" are being rewritten: after all, if the public *isn't* invited, why read the public-service announcement? Who refers to the audience as "the public" anyway?

The majority of stations now write news stories with a strong topic sentence first, rather than giving a lot of detail and not getting to the point of the story until nearly the end. There is also more of a tendency to relate the story to the listener. For example, the old style of writing would have said "At the Town Council meeting last night, by a vote of five to three, with two members abstaining, it was decided to eliminate the Q-33 bus route." The newer style would say something like "Bad news for bus riders—as of next week, there won't be a Q-33 bus anymore. That's what the Town Council decided last night."

As a consultant, who also happens to have a strong news back-ground, I'm not going to say that either style is better. I will say that if the goal of Full-Service is to *inform*, then crisp, interesting news-writing that clarifies rather than confuses is a gift to the audience. Stations need not oversimplify nor talk to the listeners as if they are ignorant, but on the other hand, some stations have taken the other extreme and been so far over the heads of the audience that no real information got through.

Newswriting today demands the same facts and important details as in years past, but the way in which it is presented can either alienate or include the average person. The most successful Full-Service stations are the ones who maintain a balance between intelligent and thoughtful reporting and a style that enables the listener to feel comfortable. Beware the pedantic approach: yes, Full-Service fans like to learn something new, but don't make them feel they've stumbled upon a college journalism seminar.

As for content of newscasts, in the past there were some very rigid rules about how many national versus how many local stories needed to be reported. Now that most stations have a network of some sort, that takes care of the national stories, but in almost all cases, the trend today seems to aim for top-of-the-mind awareness; that is, newscasts lead with whatever story the average person would care about most, be it local or national.

Sometimes, a major national story has sweeping impact, even on a local level, such as the political changes in Eastern Europe during 1989: many communities in both theUnited States and Canada have large numbers of Polish or Lithuanian people whose relatives in Europe were being affected, and they wanted to express their concerns. Major tragedies such as plane crashes also seem to temporarily occupy the topmost part of people's minds, but certain local stories can do that too. In some cities, the economy is a real issue, more real than what a political dictator in some foreign country is doing; news of some new industry coming to town bringing jobs might be a top story in those markets.

Again, it's a matter of knowing the audience and seeing the local issues through their eyes: what worries them, what concerns them, what do they want to know more about? Not every market has exciting news stories all the time, but listeners don't always come to their favorite station looking for scandal. Most come looking for a better understanding of what's happening out there, both in their hometown and in the world.

We who do journalism for a living sometimes forget that the average person, who may not read as much as people used to or be able to identify all the rulers of all the countries in Europe, still wants to be informed and especially wants to know why. Sometimes, we seem to get bogged down in the who and the where, and we assume that everybody knows as much about the world as we do, but behind the photo opportunities and the quick sound-bite style that TV popularized, there are many issues that deserve some further exploration.

Part of the Full-Service station's role as a friend often includes not just getting the story first but then relating that story to the audience in a way that sheds light on its meaning. That doesn't necessarily mean editorializing (although many stations do this to good effect), but it does mean doing a little extra work to make sure the story is clear.

For example, during the stock market problems of the late 80s, some stations interviewed local experts to explain how the decline would impact on local people. Other stations talked to small investors or did a series of brief analysis-oriented features on insider trading, junk bonds, and other issues that everyone was hearing about but perhaps not everyone fully understood.

The key is taking the time to turn the news into information, as well as finding a local angle whenever possible. Some stations with the creativity and the resources to do so actually become part of a breaking story. During the changes in Poland, a number of Full-Service stations sent their own reporters over there to provide some on-the-scene human interest about this important event.

KMOX did a unique exchange program with Moscow Radio: With glasnost being very much on people's minds, KMOX set up a discussion between two women, one in Russia, the other in St. Louis. The women talked about their daily lives, their jobs, families, budgets, etc. The first in a monthly series about life in the two countries, it was also the first time a U.S. commercial station had entered into a joint venture with a station from the Soviet Union. The discussion between the two women also included the audiences in both countries, who were able to ask questions. Robert Hyland, the founder of KMOX's information-oriented programming, saw an opportunity for his station to do more than just report on the thaw in United States–Soviet relations, and furthered KMOX's reputation as a news leader.

WHO in Des Moines also was able to become part of a news story by virtue of its relationships with presidents and former presidents. The station where Ronald Reagan was once a sportscaster was able to score a dramatic coup by having the first exclusive radio interview with President Bush. It was WHO's strong farm-news image that contributed to the arrival of the new president, who wanted to talk about his farm policy and chose WHO to have that conversation.

With regard to news today, accuracy is still foremost; a station lacking credibility can't meet the audience's need to know. Once again, more news may not be what your market wants. People may want in-depth reporting, but they may not want a half-hour news block. Further, some markets have no problem filling up a 6-minute newscast, but in other markets, after about 4 minutes, it's all been said.

Even reputable news consultants like Bruce Marr acknowledge that more isn't always better. "In some towns, there just isn't a lot of local news, and what the audience hears is filler. It may be a good idea to shorten the newscasts." That may sound ironic, coming from someone who makes his living improving the way stations do news, but Marr isn't advocating less news, nor is he saying news isn't important in the smaller markets. What he and other consultants are saying is that today's listener can tell when a station is just killing time because the log says to do 6 minutes. Sometimes it's better to re-evaluate. Three minutes of well-written important stories is more valuable to the listener than 6 minutes of boring filler. "Younger announcers may not like this," Marr says, "but it's true—the reason so many people have listened to Paul Harvey over the years is that he knows how to make the news interesting." Although not everyone can (or should) emulate a legendary personality like Paul Harvey, his techniques get excellent results, and as much as certain people who find his style anachronistic may joke about him, his ratings have repeatedly shown that people trust him and remember what he says.

In both large and small markets, Full-Service stations have benefited from having on their staff an established and well-known news reporter (who in some markets is also the news director). Just as longevity and stability have helped make certain morning-show hosts famous, these same qualities are very positive for a station's news image. A respected local newsperson has a much easier time gaining access to the important community leaders and getting some of the behind-the-scenes details of the issues. New members of a news department need to go around and make themselves known, and this process may take a while.

With news becoming more and more the primary reason why people choose a station, those stations that cover news most effectively will attract larger audience shares. Perhaps your station can't afford to send its staff to Poland, but there may be some very thought-provoking issues in your own market just waiting for someone to open a discussion. Some stations shy away from controversy for fear of offending advertisers, but at most of the successful stations, management has been able to show the sponsors the value of an objective news staff that is free to cover whatever stories it feels demand attention.

If your news staff is both responsible and reliable, it should not be forced to compromise itself to appease a client. We have all read of instances where a news team uncovered something detrimental about a local industry (perhaps it was causing excessive amounts of pollution) and that business threatened to pull all its ads from the station. In the ideal universe, this wouldn't occur, but in real life, it does. A news department must be allowed to do a credible job; its job is to report on what is happening in the area, without bias. Of course, newspeople should report something positive a client did—if that is news; but if it isn't news, the news department shouldn't operate as an unpaid publicist for any local business. Cheerleading and boosterism are necessary functions for Full-Service stations, but not necessarily as part of *news*.

The news department should have the right to do its job, and that job is to keep the audience informed about all sides of the local issues. Fortunately, the majority of advertisers today do understand that a news department must report honestly; but that doesn't mean some won't become upset if one of their products becomes the subject of an exposé (such as what occurred when a study seemed to show that oat bran was not as valuable in lowering cholesterol as cereal companies had been claiming; when some news reporters aired the study's results, they were immediately contacted by major cereal manufacturers who wanted to refute the study).

Sometimes, a controversy can turn into a very interesting debate, with intelligent spokespeople from both sides presenting their evidence and the listeners making up their own minds, but the point is, a news department should never have to espouse an approved point of view. Even KSL, which is owned by the Mormon Church, is proud of having a news department that does *not* have to get church approval for the stories it covers, nor agree with the church's views on the issues.

One other aspect of Full-Service programming deserves mention. Although weather, community service, news, and sports may make a station popular, good announcers are also a large part of the format's uniqueness. The style of today's Full-Service announcer is still a basically warm and friendly approach. Full-Service announcers don't tend to use the high-energy hyperactive style that Top-40 (and later CHR) has used, nor do Full-Service personalities talk in an artificial "radio voice." Most are known for being very conversational, much like a member of the family or a close friend. Some don't even have what would be considered a good voice, yet the way they make the audience feel comfortable compensates for that.

Today's Full-Service announcers, be they long-term veterans of the format or experienced AC or Country DJs who are just now beginning to do Full-Service, all understand their role. They are entertainers, and it is up to them to have interesting topics to discuss because they will be in the spotlight during most of their show (since so few Full-Service stations play music these days, the emphasis has switched to good conversation).

Jimmy Barrett, one of Full-Service's younger PDs, sees Full-Service as the last bastion of Personality Radio, in an era marked by tight formats and DJs who seldom spoke except to read station slogans from a file card. "Most of today's younger announcers have no idea what Full-Service is," Barrett says. While he was PD of powerhouse WJR in Detroit, he always looked for potential new members of the airstaff, so that when older members could no longer perform as they once did, someone would be prepared to step in.

It's not easy finding those people who can be the next group of Full-Service announcers. Most of today's DJs were raised with a cookie-cutter, more-music approach, and they didn't hear a lot of great personality jocks. Also, as AM radio has continued to decline, there are fewer "farm team" stations that are developing talent. More of the small stations that at one time fed the bigger ones, now are either simulcasting their FM or going to satellite. But there are some experienced announcers in other Adult formats that find Full-Service interesting and want to learn how to do it.

What does it take to become a good Full-Service announcer?

Full-service announcers are not really "announcers." They are like your best friend; they're involved with your life, they know what matters to you. The best Full-Service personalities have both relatability and topicality. They keep up with all the big issues and can easily discuss them. They also keep up with all the local events. Above all, they *read*. They read local newspapers, local magazines, whatever will keep them in touch with the community. They also attend local meetings of Kiwanis or Rotary or volunteer for social service committees. They literally become an active member of the community, and that makes them sound more natural when they talk about it.

Barrett has one other reminder: "Good Full-Service announcers talk *to* the audience, not *at* them." Earl McDaniel of KSSK in Honolulu expands on that theme: "Good Full-Service announcers know how to communicate and how to be intelligent. But they also know how to have fun doing their job." Robert Hyland of KMOX says that whether an announcer is in a small market or a large one, Full-Service radio requires a long-term commitment. "Be very serious about doing it well. We need informed announcers who respect the audience." Rick Sellers of WMT tells his announcers to

> . . . use their mind as well as their mouth. Their job is to empathize with the listener. Good announcers should be able to think on their feet—if an interesting opportunity presents itself, they should know how to seize that opportunity. Our staff is constantly reaching out to the audience; if we hear about a charitable event, we call and offer our help. I ask my air staff to give the audience reasons to listen. Good announcers should evaluate their own shows by asking themselves "why would I listen to this?" and "am I local enough?" and "could people get this information anywhere?" Our announcers know that this isn't just a "job." It requires maturity to do Full-Service well.

David Bernstein, who went from WTIC to WBZ, instructs his airstaff to

> . . . teach me something; tell me something I didn't know before. After an announcer has said something, the listener should be able to respond "thanks for telling me that!" This doesn't mean we're educational radio, but it does mean

that the announcer shouldn't waste the listener's time with filler. I want the audience to feel that we always give them useful information.

So if becoming a successful Full-Service announcer takes time and requires preparation and hard work, why do it? The majority of experienced Full-Service personalities are men and women who have become attached to a particular community and truly enjoy living there. Some may have been Top-40 DJs years ago, but they see themselves as capable of much more than just playing the hits. They like being active in their community, and they gain great satisfaction making a difference in people's lives. They don't think of themselves as old, whatever their chronological age: they love radio and they want to continue doing it. Full-Service announcers also realize that personality isn't wanted in certain other formats, so they very much welcome the opportunity to be entertainers; and, in all honesty, they also have a good time being local celebrities around their market.

The other important part of doing Full-Service is an area that many PDs might question, yet especially in smaller markets, this aspect has as great an influence on the station as the programming: the sales department. In music-intensive formats, sales and programming have at times regarded each other with animosity. PDs wanted to play more hits, account executives wanted to sell more commercials. PDs didn't like sales remotes, sales managers felt PDs should be more cooperative, and so it went. PDs began doing commercial-free hours, which sales managers disliked because that implied commercials were negative and the absence of them was positive. Yes, PDs understood that commercials helped pay their salary, and they really did want to be perceived as team players. Still, when the general manager wanted to increase the number of commercial minutes per hour, few PDs thought that was good news.

In Top-40's and AOR's early years, the role of the PD wasn't considered management at some stations; the PD was more like the head DJ. He (and it almost always was a he) scheduled the air staff, did station promo's, picked the music (along with the music director), thought up great ideas for contests, and usually did an air shift, as well as critiquing the other announcers. PDs back then could wear jeans and a T-shirt to work. The job may not have had a lot of autonomy, but the benefits often included free records, tickets to rock concerts, and the opportunity to meet all the groups. And it was certainly a more enjoyable job than most people had.

As competition increased and more stations were fighting for the advertising dollars, rock radio became more of a business. It could still be fun, but now PDs were program managers, and programming was no longer a bunch of educated guesses. PDs at many stations were expected to know some law (is our latest contest planned out thoroughly so that we can't be sued for fraud?), some motivation, and even publicity. Some PDs were sent to management seminars to improve their skills. Others learned more about sales. Some PDs became so adept at the over-all workings of a station that they went on to become general managers.

Gradually, PDs and general sales managers (GSMs) found themselves working together much more often, planning strategies, and ex-changing ideas. PDs wanted big prizes for contests; GSMs wanted announcers who would willingly appear at a client's store. As PDs became part of the management team, their point of view was listened to by the sales staff, and vice versa. Although it would be facile to say that all the problems between PDs and sales departments at rock stations were resolved, it is true that taking the PD more seriously led to a spirit of compromise.

At Full-Service stations, there had not been the same sort of history of tension between sales and programming as was seen in music-intensive stations. Of course, PDs had their clashes with sales ("What do you mean we have to do three remotes on Saturday?"), but the lines of distinction were not so sharply drawn. For one thing, at many small-market stations (and even some larger ones), members of the programming staff also did some selling. For another, in lower-paying markets, appearing at a remote was a good way for an announcer to make some extra money. Since the commitment of Full-Service included being extremely visible in the community, the entire station participated in one way or other. It was difficult to resent a sales manager who spent long hours visiting clients and also represented the station at Rotary or Lions.

At Full-Service, the roles often mingled. Newspeople shook hands with merchants, announcers covered news meetings when the news staff couldn't, account executives got information for public-service announcements, and everybody attended station functions in the community. At the small stations in particular, the owner was often someone with ties to the area, and so were many of the staff. As a result, just about everyone knew the merchants and the civic leaders, and the station was seen as an extension of the town itself. This fostered a feeling of accessibility and friendship, which in turn created a good climate for sales.

Even now, the reports of AM's decline don't upset the account executives at many small-market stations: there are still a number of unrated markets in both the United States and Canada, and sales staffs who have never become dependent on using ratings information are free to sell the old-fashioned way, with solid relationships in the business community and a service-oriented attitude.

Even rated markets are finding that having (or not having) big numbers is no automatic guarantee of sales success. "The problem," explains Dianne Gleason, general manager of KOTA in Rapid City, South Dakota, "is that so many of the agencies have young buyers, and they don't understand what Full-Service does. Even though it's difficult to sell this format, local merchants will tell you that Full-Service gets them excellent results."

Meanwhile, Full-Service giants like WGN bill more than any other Chicago station, AM or FM; and in medium markets, both WHO and WMT show excellent profits, even with heavy competition from other stations. It is true that some AM stations have had some hard times; it is also true that others are alive and healthy on the financial side. Not all of them are the WBZs and the KMOXs; some successful AMs are in markets like Yankton, South Dakota.

Dean Sorenson owns a group of stations in five midwestern states. Among them are some community Full-Service AMs. Few of his stations are in rated markets, but he doesn't feel that is a liability. Rather, he prefers to operate stations in towns with 11,000 to 17,000 residents; he feels closer relationships can be forged in these towns. He also feels selling with ratings alone isn't the mark of a good salesperson. "We believe sales is a career. There are no short hours or easy hours. We've got some people at our stations who have been working side by side with local merchants for years."

Sorenson gives his GSMs and account executives extensive sales training and recommends that they take a Dale Carnegie course as well. He is proud of the fact that local merchants trust and respect his stations. "I think too many people sell gimmicks instead of building the credibility of radio in the eyes of the buyer for the long-term."

Although Sorenson's stations are very much client-centered, they are also community-centered, as traditional Full-Service has always been. "Our stations are all a part of their community. If there's a parade or a store opening, we're there. And if there's a meeting, our newsperson is sitting in the front row, taking notes and getting tape for the next newscast. We are always there, and I think it makes a difference."

Dean Sorenson is known for how profitable his small AMs are. Even though he also owns some FMs, he still believes a well-run AM station that actively serves its community can make money.

As for the future, some AM stations are hopeful that technological advances will bring a continuous-band radio to the forefront. Since many listeners under 35 years old grew up entirely with FM and have seldom switched over to the AM band, a continuous-band radio would make switching unnecessary; with AM and FM equally available, younger listeners tuning across the band could very easily find a Full-Service station they might not have sampled otherwise.

As for music, stations are taking a wait-and-see attitude. Most are eliminating it or restricting it to weekends (or to special theme shows), but some stations still find, as WGY did, that local research indicates a preference for a blend of information, news, and music. Most consultants expect the AM band to be all talk, but individual stations should do what works in their market.

The old saying "if it ain't broke, don't fix it" applies here. Although KMOX does well with mostly all talk and features, that may not be right for your market. With the aging of the AM listener, Top-40 probably won't make a comeback on AM in the near future (although a few AM music formats have worked, such as Big Band), but that doesn't necessarily mean music on AM is doomed in every market. If WLW, WTIC, and KDKA (among others) still find music a useful element, it may be useful in other places too, although clearly the days of music as the *only* element have passed.

On the other hand, some FM stations are now increasing the services they offer. Where sports on FM used to be rare, now some stations do carry some, and some ACs are expanding the amount of information they offer, especially in morning drive. It seems a matter of time before FM stations begin doing some form of Full-Service.

The best AMs, meanwhile, are refusing to project an old image. Although it may be difficult to replace retiring legends like Bob Steele or Wally Phillips, WTIC and WGN have dealt with this issue and still manage to hold on to their audience.

AMs are also examining the balance between bringing in enough revenue and having too many commercials. Some AMs, WMAL among them, run in excess of 15 commercial minutes an hour (in morning drive, some reach 18). This has contributed to the perception that AM is all talk and clutter, while FM is "more music, less talk." (That, by the way, is changing.) Several researchers have found that anything over 12 minutes is a tune-out. AM Full-Service has the advantage of its excellent personality announcers, many of whom are masterful at doing live commercials in such a way that it seems like information. However, too much of anything can become a problem, and some AMs are trying to develop strategies that will get the necessary business done effectively, while still keeping the station's programming moving along smoothly.

Consultant Don Benson, executive vice president of Burkhart/Douglas and Associates, says

> What makes a Full-Service station successful is consistency and personality. People know that if there's a disaster, like an earthquake, they can turn to a Full-Service station and get all the details. The stations that win with this format have announcers who aren't offensive—they're informative, but they never do any material that is in bad taste. It's a neighborly style of radio. The biggest challenge for Full-Service is gradually introducing new air talent—don't wait till the current staff dies. Groom your new people so the audience can get used to them. Also, keep sounding contemporary. Full-Service may attract an older audience, but that doesn't mean they want a boring station. Be creative. Invest in your people and keep seeking out the events that really matter to your community. This is a very long-term format, but if it's done well, it can show strong growth. I definitely don't believe AM radio is dead.

David Oakes, vice president of research for Joint Communications, has a somewhat different opinion. Although he agrees that some Full-Service stations on AM are quite prosperous, he sees trouble ahead.

> Obviously, personality is the big reason why AM Full-Service wins. But the problem is when these amazing entertainers retire, you have to quickly replace them with someone equally good, or else you lose continuity. Heritage alone won't hold the audience if a station lacks the great personalities. Actually, Full-Service on AM is the backlash against fragmentation. While everyone else is narrowcasting, Full-Service says "you *can* have it all on one station—news, music, sports, all of it." But unfortunately for Full-Service, AM radio is fighting an uphill battle, and as a result, AM Full-Service is holding on for dear life. Fragmentation has changed everything over the past 20 years. The younger demographics will not listen to AM. These people have a shorter attention span, and they get bored quickly. In fact, when Full-Service does switch over to FM, and it will, the FM version will have to take into account what today's younger listeners want, and FM Full-Service won't have as much talk or news or information as AM does. The heritage stations like WJR will continue to win because they have top-of-the-mind awareness, thanks to their news image and all the

charities they work with. But I expect even more fragmentation on AM, and it will be difficult for any new stations on the AM band to do Full-Service.

Whichever view you subscribe to, Full-Service stations continue to defy most predictions made about them. Many of the heritage stations keep showing up in the top three in the ratings, book after book. Critics can say that's just because they have famous call letters, yet a number of these stations are even managing to attract some of those elusive younger listeners. Although KMOX and WCCO won't ever be number one with teens, their listeners aren't all in nursing homes either. Consultant Jim Smith suggests that

> Perhaps the truth lies somewhere in the middle. WGN is a good example of a station that keeps entertaining the audience. Research repeatedly shows that people of all ages love their personalities. They even attract the under thirty-five listeners that AM isn't supposed to get. I don't think there's a simple formula; it's more a matter of making the audience comfortable. The audiences of the great stations expect great things from them. But even that isn't the key to their success. Full-Service stations are successful because they remind the older listeners of the Golden Age of Radio, because Full-Service involves itself with all the service elements just like radio used to. The younger listeners find it when they want news and information, but for the most part, the majority of Full-Service listeners will be from the older demographics. They can really relate to this style of radio. The point is that Full-Service is a foreground format, and if I were in sales, I would stress that fact. Full-Service lends itself to being listened to very closely. It's definitely not a jukebox.

With so many radio listeners feeling that most stations today sound alike, with FM no longer being seen as creative and unique, and with more new stations still going on the air in small and medium markets, the next few years should be very interesting for trend-watchers. Research shows that radio listening is very strong in the morning. It also shows that young adults don't read as much as they did a generation ago, and estimates are that one out of every five Americans reads at a fourth-grade level, with one out of eleven being functionally illiterate. If that is so, then both TV and radio news will continue to benefit. Although attention spans may be shorter, the need for information is still very present. Full-Service has been there since the beginning, raising money for charity, saluting good citizens, offering a wide variety of programming from talk shows to radio drama, playing a variety of music, and entertaining the listeners with outstanding personalities. Today, when mature and interesting announcers are difficult to find in certain markets, many Full-Service stations are still doing their best to present them; making the job easier has been the resurgence of the networks.

For a while, after the Golden Age of Radio ended and TV stole many of the networks' best shows, the main role the networks filled for Adult radio was to offer news on the hour. In the 80s, however, renewed interest in the networks occurred for the many AM stations seeking talk shows or special features. Suddenly, it was possible to hear a big-name expert, even in a small town, thanks to services such as

Monday - Friday

Town and Country Time — Five Live!
5:00 - 7:00 A.M.

5:00 a.m.	CBS and WMT News		6:30 a.m.	WMT Weather - Greg Story
5:09 a.m.	Daily Devotions		6:34 a.m.	WMT News - Jim Boyd
5:30 a.m.	WMT Weatherbriefs		6:40 a.m.	Agribusiness News/Markets
5:35 a.m.	Mutual Sports		6:55 a.m.	WMT Weatherbriefs
6:00 a.m.	CBS News		6:57 a.m.	WMT Sportsbriefs - Ron Gonder
6:06 a.m.	WMT Newsbriefs		7:00 a.m.	CBS "World News Round-Up"
6:07 a.m.	WMT Weatherbriefs		7:15 a.m.	WMT Weather
6:09 a.m.	CBS Business News		7:16 a.m.	WMT News
6:11 a.m.	Farm Markets - Rich Balvanz		7:25 a.m.	CBS "The Osgood File"
6:25 a.m.	CBS "The Osgood File"			

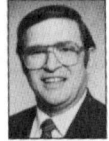

Jerry Passer
Farm Director

Rich Balvanz
Farm Editor

The Musical Clock with Jerry Carr
7:30 - 10:00 A.M.

7:30 a.m.	WMT Weather		8:55 a.m.	WMT Sports
7:35 a.m.	The Musical Clock		8:59 a.m.	WMT News
7:55 a.m.	WMT Sports		9:00 a.m.	CBS News
8:00 a.m.	CBS and WMT News		9:06 a.m.	WMT Weather
8:15 a.m.	WMT Weather		9:25 a.m.	CBS "The Osgood File"
8:18 a.m.	Your Money Minute		9:30 a.m.	Opening Farm Markets
8:25 a.m.	CBS "The Osgood File"		9:56 a.m.	WMT News
8:40 a.m.	"Let's Have A Word"			

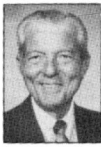

Jerry Carr

The Gary Edwards Show
10:00 A.M. - 3:00 P.M.
Featuring The Open Line Recipe Exchange Show, 1:00 P.M.- 2:00 P.M.

10:00 a.m.	CBS News		12:10 p.m.	Bus. News/Stock Market Rpt.-Jim Doyne
10:06 a.m.	WMT Weather		12:15 p.m.	WMT News
10:28 a.m.	Joblines		12:25 p.m.	CBS Feature: "Correspondent's Notebook"
10:30 a.m.	Agri-Market Update		12:28 p.m.	Report to Consumers
10:40 a.m.	Doggone Bulletin Board-Lost/Found Pets			(fr. the Editors of **Consumer Reports**)
10:56 a.m.	WMT News		12:30 p.m.	Farm Markets/News/Information
11:00 a.m.	CBS News		1:00 p.m.	CBS News
11:06 a.m.	WMT Weather		1:06 p.m.	WMT Weather
11:25 a.m.	CBS Feature: "Health Talk"		1:08 p.m.	Household Hints & Recipe Exchange
11:35 a.m.	WMT Weather		1:30 p.m.	Closing Farm Markets
11:40 a.m.	WMT Sports		2:00 p.m.	CBS News
11:45 a.m.	Agribusiness News		2:06 p.m.	WMT Weather
11:55 a.m.	Farm Markets		2:25 p.m.	CBS "Cronkite 20th Century"
12:00 Noon	CBS News		2:56 p.m.	WMT News
12:06 p.m.	WMT Weather			

Gary Edwards

▶ *Figure 4* This partial programming schedule from WMT, Cedar Rapids, Iowa, is indicative of a Full-Service program schedule. Used with permission from WMT AM 600 Radio, Cedar Rapids, Iowa.

The Steve Carpenter Show
3:00 - 8:00 P.M.
Featuring Project 600, 6:30 - 8:00 P.M.

3:00 p.m.	CBS News
3:06 p.m.	WMT Weather
3:56 p.m.	WMT News
4:00 p.m.	CBS News
4:06 p.m.	WMT Weather
4:25 p.m.	WMT Sports
5:00 p.m.	WMT Afternoon Edition - CBS News
5:06 p.m.	WMT News
5:20 p.m.	Stock Market Report
5:22 p.m.	WMT Weather
5:25 p.m.	WMT Sports
5:40 p.m.	Sports Flashback
5:45 p.m.	CBS Feature: "Dan Rather Reporting"
5:50 p.m.	CBS Feature: "News Notes"
5:54 p.m.	Report to Consumers (fr. the Editors of **Consumer Reports**)
6:00 p.m.	CBS News: "The World Tonight"
6:10 p.m.	WMT News, Weather
6:15 p.m.	CBS SPORTSTIME - Brent Musburger
6:20 p.m.	Farm Review
6:24 p.m.	Today in Business
6:27 p.m.	Joblines
6:30 p.m.	Project 600 - Telephone Talk and Features
7:00 p.m.	CBS News
7:06 p.m.	WMT Weather
7:55 p.m.	WMT News

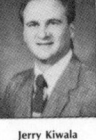

Steve Carpenter

The Overnight Show with Jerry Kiwala
8:00 P.M. - 5:00 A.M.
Featuring The Larry King Show, 10:00 P.M. - 3:00 A.M.

8:00 p.m.	CBS News
8:06 p.m.	WMT Weatherbriefs
8:07 p.m.	Telephone, Talk & Music - Jerry Kiwala "End of the Road" - Tom Bodett (Fri. Only)
9:00 p.m.	WMT Weatherbriefs
9:01 p.m.	"For The People" - Chuck Harder
9:55 p.m.	WMT News
10:00 p.m.	CBS News
10:06 p.m.	The Larry King Show
10:28 p.m.	WMT Sports
10:50 p.m.	Prep Scores Report (Tues. and Fri. during high school football and basketball seasons)
10:43 p.m.	The Larry King Show
11:00 p.m.	CBS News
11:06 p.m.	The Larry King Show
11:30 p.m.	WMT Weather
12:00 Mid.	CBS News
12:28 a.m.	WMT Weather
1:00 a.m.	CBS News
1:06 a.m.	The Larry King Show
1:30 a.m.	WMT Weather
2:00 a.m.	CBS News
2:06 a.m.	The Larry King Show
2:28 a.m.	WMT Weather
3:00 a.m.	CBS News
3:06 a.m.	WMT Weather
3:08 a.m.	Nightline - Jerry Kiwala
4:00 a.m.	CBS News
4:06 a.m.	America in the Morning (Tues. - Fri.) The Week in Review (Sat. only)
4:30 a.m.	Mutual News
4:35 a.m.	CBS Newsmark (Sat. only)

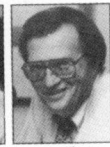

Jerry Kiwala

Chuck Harder   Larry King

"Talk-Net." Network talk shows have toll-free phone numbers so that listeners from anywhere can call in. Many Full-Service stations have their own personalities on during the day, and go to their network at night (much as was done in the golden age).The positive side of this is, of course, stations that could never afford a celebrity talk show now have one nightly; the downside is that so many stations now air Bruce Williams or Larry King that AM in many markets has no local programming anywhere.

Still, AM Full-Service is continuing its commitment to inform and entertain. Since the format is so flexible, it can accommodate a network show or develop one of its own. Full-Service will certainly encounter many new challenges in the 90s, but it's safe to say that it will remain true to its original goal, serving the community and upholding the tradition of "radio in the public interest."

9
Some Do's and Don'ts in Today's Full-Service

What follows is a summation of what makes a Full-Service station successful. Although there are no magic answers for any format (this especially holds true for Full-Service), these basic rules will be useful to any prospective owner trying to build a new Full-Service or to anyone going to work at an established station.

1. *Be proud of your community.* Full-Service radio, even in a major market, is community radio. Whether you are in Keene, New Hampshire, or Los Angeles, California, seek out and find the positives about your area and let people know about them. Remember that people who live in a community have a reason for doing so. Even if the town seems rather bleak to you, use the power of your station to create a better image for the area. I've seen stations literally jump in and rescue a town's economy by embarking on a public-relations campaign along with the town merchants and civic groups to express pride, as well as to help improve the quality of life there. Full-Service is radio that can really make an impact.

2. *Take on the challenge.* Whether it's convincing people that AM isn't dead or that your town has great benefits, raising money for a local charity, or helping to fight teenage drug-use, what's life without a challenge? Full-Service has taken on many of them and gotten results. Plan your strategy, and then go for it!

3. *Plan your work, then work your plan.* An old cliché, but still true. Years ago, when there was little competition, stations could try anything (so long as it was legal) and not lose the audience. Today, listeners have so many choices that guessing isn't an effective way to program. Before you begin anything, whether it's a new contest or a strategic attack on a competitor, sit down and plan it out, step by step. Managers who are organized tend to be more effective, because fewer details will fall through the cracks. Most successful stations have a promotions director or at least a calendar of events so that they are able to spread their promotions out and not place events so close together that they lose their impact.

4. *Don't be the Lone Ranger.* Many good ideas are ruined because one person fails to tell anyone what the plan is; this creates confusion as the only person who did know about it tries to carry it out, to everyone else's surprise. As good a manager as your station has, and as much as you feel secrecy is desirable when planning strategy, the people who are going to be involved in implementing the plan should have the opportunity to provide some input. Management by committee seldom works, but management by letting people find out about it later doesn't work either, and

causes resentment. Have one final decision-maker, but let the other department heads and team members offer their points of view; sometimes they can see flaws or think of more effective ways to accomplish the goal.

5. *Communicate with the team.* Yes, there is a team. As in sports, the players may not like each other personally, but when they work together as a unit, the team is more likely to win. If your station policy gives all the bonuses and extra benefits to sales and nothing to programming, that's asking for problems. If you don't have regular department head meetings, if you only talk to your engineer after something breaks, if you only see staff members when you want to criticize something they did, chances are the station's communication isn't all it could be. To win in today's competitive arena, everyone must feel included in some way. Make sure each player knows his or her role; give team members the training they need to perform effectively, but definitely encourage a team spirit.

6. *Know your audience; never assume.* Just when you think it's safe to do it the way you always did it in the past, along comes a new competitor, or three stations in town change format. The reality is that circumstances are always changing: people move into the neighborhood, kids grow up and leave for college, your best announcer retires, your top biller decides to take a job in Los Angeles. Even if yours is a stable station with legendary call letters, the issues that concern the audi-ence now may not have crossed anyone's mind 10 years ago (I can recall when the word "pregnant" was not allowed on the "I Love Lucy" show; contrast that to the tabloid TV shows of the late 80s, with their graphic discussions of safe sex practices).

Keep listening to the people in your market. Join the important civic and service groups and really attend some of their meetings. Do some person-in-the-street interviews or some people polls so that you can get a feel for public opinion. Talk to area merchants, not just to sell them advertising but to become more familiar with what they want and what concerns them. Make sure your station is considered a **fair, honest** sounding board for people's views, and strive to help the audience to understand the issues better. Above all, don't make assumptions about what people want based on what they used to want: times may have changed.

7. *Be visible in your community.* Dean Sorenson was right. Whether it's a parade or a store opening, if it affects a number of people in your town, be there. Make sure your newspeople have business cards and microphone shields so that whenever they represent the station, they can display the call letters. Even if nothing major gets decided at the town meetings, the fact that somebody from the station attended says that you care. Make sure that everyone who represents the station out in the community dresses in a professional manner and conveys a positive image. Have a banner to take to events. If you're a major-market station, you already have all the fancy items (vans, mobile studios, hot-air balloons), but make sure you have enough little handouts (pens, key chains, teddy bears for the kids with the station logo on the bear's shirt) for people to take home with them. You and I may be tired of these things, but the average person thinks they're cute, and they serve the purpose of keeping the call letters in front of the person. Whenever possible, things for kids go over very well; just make sure the item in question is safe.

RELATABLES TEST

If you can name a "best" or recognized "favorite" in each category, you're in touch with your market and can really serve your listeners.

MEDIA
- TV Station _____
- Radio Station _____
  - AM _____
  - FM _____
  - Talk Show _____
- TV Anchor - Male _____
- TV Anchor - Female _____
- Newspaper Columnist _____
- Disc Jockey _____
- Sportscaster _____
- Weatherman _____
- Ad Agency _____
- Local Advertisement _____
- Ad Campaign _____
- Magazine _____

GOODS/SERVICES
- Department Store _____
- Furniture Store _____
- Health/Athletic _____
- Men's/Ladies' Shop _____
- Car Dealer _____
- Newsstand _____
- Drug Store _____
- Alterations/Cleaner _____
- Travel Agency _____
- Hotel _____

FOOD/DRINK
- Restaurant (overall) _____
- Restaurant Atmosphere _____
- Restaurant Service _____
- Burger _____
- Mexican _____
- Cuban _____
- Pizza _____
- Seafood _____
- Ribs _____
- Italian _____
- French _____
- Chinese _____
- Steak _____
- Raw Bar _____
- Salad Bar _____
- Bar _____
- Happy Hour _____

ENTERTAINMENT
- Attraction _____
- Place to Dance _____
- Arts Event _____
- Beach/Lake _____
- Best Thing to Happen to (town) _____
- Best Place to Watch People _____
- Best Place to Meet People _____
- Best Freebie _____

PEOPLE
- Local Hero _____
- Local Politician _____
- Best Looking Male _____
- Best Looking Female _____

MISCELLANEOUS
- Suburb _____
- New building _____
- Bargain _____
- Romantic Spot _____
- Weekend Getaway _____

▶ *Figure 5* Show preparation is the most important time air talent can spend. To help DJs, Shane Media Service has developed this "Relatables Test," an attempt to call attention to landmarks and services which people in that market talk about. Used with permission from Ed Shane, President, Shane Media Services.

Promotional goodies cost money, but the investment in goodwill is often worth the expense. Any useful item that has your station's logo on it, such as beach towels or umbrellas or coffee mugs, keeps promoting long after your van has left.

If you can't afford promotional items, being there is the next best thing. Know what the important events are in your area and make sure you are seen. WHO has its own building at the Iowa State Fair, and millions of people see the station there. Many stations broadcast live from state fairs for that very reason. If your community doesn't have a lot of events, create one and invite people!

8. *Be their best friend.* Do the little things. Have staff hand out balloons at a children's hospital. Make sure the audience can get the most up-to-date weather forecasts whenever they need to know. If weather is not an issue in your market (in Hawaii and Puerto Rico, for example, the weather stays the same—pleasant—for weeks at a time), then something else is. Maybe it's traffic. Maybe it's stock market reports or farm news. Whatever it is, be the best source for it, and let them know you have it for them. Let them know where they can take the kids this weekend, or where they can save some money. Have a consumer advocate to answer their questions about defective products. If you have the budget, create a "Call to Action" show that helps the average person cut through red tape and finds solutions. Above all be friendly when they call, and try to answer their letters.

9. *Be interesting.* That sounds like a truism, but you'd be amazed how many stations still offer filler instead of substance. Not everyone has a huge budget or can afford to pay large salaries, but a station can still offer listeners programs that are worth their time. In smaller markets, some of the networks and syndicators have some good shows, but also use the resources in the community. Create useful short programs such as KMA has done for years, using local experts to answer a daily question about health or fitness or gardening or the stock market or whatever are the topics of concern in your area. Some stations run shows about car repair or answer questions about pets. Teach the audience something new, but do it in an entertaining

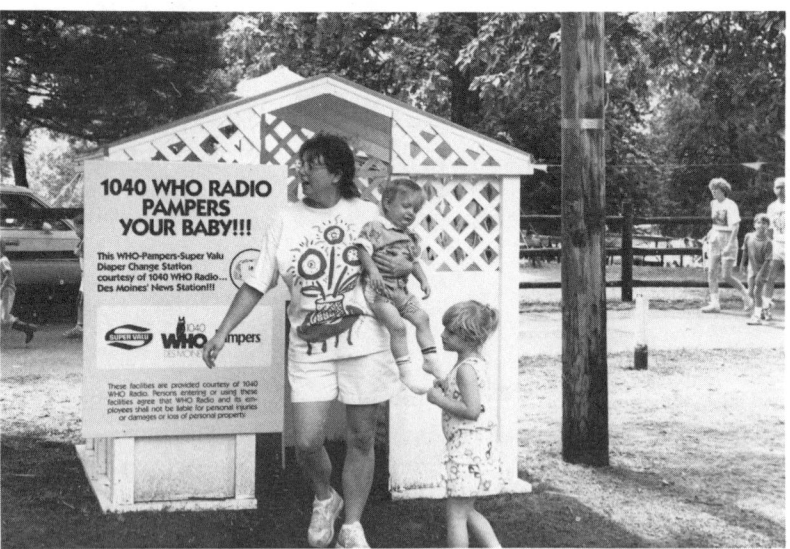

▶ *Figure 6* *A Des Moines, Iowa Full-Service radio station "pampers" its listeners. Used with permission from WHO 1040 Radio, Des Moines, Iowa.*

manner. Reading something verbatim from the wire service is probably not as interesting as using the wire copy as a guide and asking a local expert to expand upon the theme. Just because a show has a sponsor doesn't mean it's a good program; wherever possible, PDs and GSMs need to discuss these matters so that both are satisfied and the audience doesn't end up bored.

10. *Give the audience variety.* Even at the talk-oriented stations, they know it's best to offer variety. Some talk shows are serious, while others are in a lighter vein. Being serious all the time can become overwhelming for the listener. Feel free to talk about the depressing subjects, because they are a part of life and many people have opinions about them, but also make time for celebrity news, movie reviews, comedy, old-time radio dramas (many of which are now back in syndication and sound quite good), or music. Keep the balance between informing and entertaining: *both* are important.

11. *Be the best station in your market.* Just because a station serves only 8000 people doesn't mean it has to sound amateurish. Have high standards and encourage the staff to attain them. Operate with a winning attitude: the listeners don't read *Billboard* or *Broadcasting* very often, so they may not have heard the rumor that AM radio is dead. Give them a station they can trust and rely on, and who knows, they just might remain loyal to it!

12. *Communicate naturally with the audience.* As we discussed in Chapter 8, there has been a shift in how news is read and written, as well as in the way announcers relate. The key today is to be *conversational.* You can deliver a serious story in the appropriate manner, but today's Full-Service announcers never talk down to the listener. Get to the point, give the details, but make sure you are clarifying rather than confusing the issues.

Use actualities when you can, but only if they give a story more impact: long, boring sound bites sound like you're trying to fill up space. If your news- or sportscasts drag on too long, shorten them—you want quality, not quantity. Remember people's shorter attention span, and know when you've spent enough time on a subject. Ask guests intelligent questions: it sheds no light on anything when you ask ball players how they felt about losing the game. If your friends were sitting with this person, what sorts of information would they want?

Be contemporary in your on-air delivery. Too many announcers still speak in old radio clichés: "It's about 25 minutes before the hour of 3 o'clock." Would you really tell time that way to a friend, or would you say "It's 25 minutes of three?" Why say "Today's weather calls for rain" when weather can't call? Also temperatures don't read, and barometers don't stand. ("The temperature reading is 23 degrees outside.") At the end of your show, do you say, "Well, that's it for me" (which sounds as if you're off to face a firing squad) or "Well, I'm out of here" (which sounds as if you hate your job and can't wait to leave)? Then there are the verbal crutches like "music from" and "coming up next," which when said over and over during a shift make you sound like a robot. Eliminating artificial phrases makes you sound more real. Radio clichés aren't fatal, but an entire show filled with them keeps announcers from sounding like a friend to the audience. Even experienced announcers need to have someone critique them periodically to make sure they are sounding conversational.

13. *Respect your heritage, but don't worship it.* Even the original Full-Service giants like KDKA have had to eliminate some of the features they used to run and play different music. Yes, the audience wants consistency and continuity, but your station shouldn't be a living tribute to 1936. Some long-running shows still sound current even 50 years later, while others sound out of place on a modern station. Evaluate your features regularly. Also evaluate your jingles, your liners, your positioning statements. Build on the traditions you've established over the years, but remember that tradition alone won't make you number one. Some Full-Service stations are able to be all things to all people, block programming a wide range of programs for people from 8 to 80 years old, but most stations don't have that luxury. Serve your target audience well, let the listeners know they can count on you, but don't be afraid to make some modifications if doing so will improve your sound.

14. *Don't try to be something you're not.* No one will deny that KMOX or WSB are legendary radio stations and that they do some amazing things, but the world doesn't need a thousand clones of them. It's fine to strive for excellence, but that doesn't mean becoming a carbon copy of some other station. Just because WCCO did it doesn't mean it will work for you. I've seen too many stations become followers when they should have been leaders. Learn from the great stations, but carve your own niche.

15. *Don't be afraid of consultants.* Not because I am one, but let's face it: when you're at a station every day, it can be difficult to maintain objectivity. There are some very reputable consultants who will give you an unbiased point of view, as well as some useful advice. The same goes for sales trainers, management seminars, and NAB or RAB workshops. You don't have to agree with everything that is said in these places, but hearing other opinions is one good way to avoid getting into a rut.

16. *Don't look for the magic answer.* Full-Service is a format that takes time to earn listener respect. Achieving credibility with your audience won't happen overnight, especially if you once had it but then lost it. Be willing to work hard to get the audience and the advertisers to believe in you, but don't be surprised if there aren't any shortcuts.

17. *Don't forget to say "thank you."* It's amazing how those of us in the communications industry often fail to communicate. Do your salespeople send thank-you notes to clients? Do they express their gratitude for the client's business? Does your station have a mechanism for thanking listeners, especially people who have done good things for the community? Do the managers at your station acknowledge the hard work of the staff? Some managers find it easier to criticize than to praise. Sometimes it's very necessary to confront negative staff behaviors, but it's just as necessary to reward positive ones. People don't just work for the money; they work for the appreciation too. Make sure they feel appreciated when they've performed well for you. From the receptionist up to the general manager, everyone enjoys a kind word. Don't take your staff for granted.

18. *Don't let yourself become mentally lazy.* Maybe you don't like to read, but reading can provide you with some excellent ideas and strategies. As I mentioned elsewhere, sales and management people should read *American Demographics* magazine for its wealth of important sales research. Some good magazines about current events include *The New Republic, Washington Monthly, Mother Jones,* and *The Utne Reader.* In addition to newspapers and weekly news magazines, newspeople might find both *Washington Journalism Review,* and *Columbia Journalism Review* of value. Music magazines like *Rolling Stone* and industry publications like *The Record, Billboard,* and *Radio & Records* are informational whether you play music or not: if you want to do celebrity reports or discuss trends in popular music, you may as well keep up with what is being written about the state of the industry. There are also good ideas in industry monthly magazines like *Radio Only.*

As for some books that I have recommended to managers, *Positioning: The Battle for Your Mind* by Ries and Trout is, of course, still useful. So is *Success with the Gentle Art of Verbal Self-Defense* by Suzette Elgin. I also like *Dinosaur Brains: Dealing with All Those Impossible People at Work,* by Albert Bernstein; also *Zen to Go*, a collection of wonderful motivational quotes edited by Jon Winokur. For anyone at your station whose life has been affected by an alcoholic or an addict, buy that person a copy of *Co-Dependent No More* by Melody Beattie, as well as *Home Away from Home: The Art of Self-Sabotage* by Janet Woititz. Whatever you think of reading, make some time for it. It's well worth the effort!

19. *Don't ignore your engineer.* Many stations can't afford the latest state-of-the-art gadgets, but it's self-defeating if you don't give the audience good technical quality. Keep your equipment well-maintained, and plan ahead for emergencies: if you live in a climate that has major storms, do you have an auxiliary power supply so that you can still broadcast to all those people who are listening on their transistor radio when their electricity has gone off? Stations with no backup generator often wish they had one during a crisis. Do you and your engineer speak often so that he or she can do preventative maintenance? There are AMs that are known for having superb audio. It's in your best interest to be one of those.

20. *Don't give up on Full-Service.* Okay, it can be expensive, it can be difficult to sell sometimes, and it's not easy to find announcers who know how to do it, but it's also an incredibly rewarding format, one that can keep the business community healthy while keeping the average person entertained. Full-Service can save lives, it can put a town on the map, and contrary to what some cynics may tell you, if you and your staff have the enthusiasm and the commitment, it *can* be profitable.

In many cities, in unrated markets and Top-5 markets, Full-Service stations are doing some of the most creative and exciting radio. It's a format with enormous resilience and flexibility. It may not get huge ratings in every city, but it does get a very devoted and vocal audience, which, according to demographers, has money to spend and doesn't mind spending it. Yes, sometimes you have to do some public relations (or consciousness-raising) on certain agencies who think an older audience is negative, but with the entire population moving into those older demographics, Full-Service could turn out to be the safest format of all in the next few years.

21. (And perhaps the most important of all) *Don't lose your sense of humor!* AM radio definitely has its problems as we enter the 1990s. Yet in spite of that, there are numerous AM Full-Service success stories, and not all of them are the heritage stations, as we have seen. You can't avoid the problems and the challenges, but bear in mind that FMs, TV and newspaper are facing tougher competition too. Having an FM signal is no longer a guarantee of success, not when there are markets with more than 20 stations to chose from (and so-called small markets where there are as many as 12 radio stations, three TV stations, plus all the cable channels). So keep smiling. There are still a lot of possibilities out there, and it's better to be amused than to be angry about it all. There is actual research which shows that humor is good for you. So, have you had your daily laugh yet?

There are other do's and don't's of a more personal nature. Among them are *do keep yourself healthy, do solve your problems instead of just complaining about them,* and *don't put off the things you know you need to do.* Although these won't ensure your success in Full-Service, they will make you more effective. People who are too stressed out have a difficult time making good management decisions. In this overly competitive society of ours, you need to be at your best, physically and mentally, or your competition may leave you behind. In your effort to build your own career and make your station number one, don't forget your family and your religion, both of which can offer you encouragement and support.

To sum it all up, Full-Service radio has filled a void for many people. It has been a reliable source of information, as well as a good friend. In no other format can an announcer become as close with the audience; in few other formats can a salesperson have so much positive impact on an entire community. If, as the doomsayers foretell, we are about to see the end of AM Full-Service, I am one of those who will feel we have really lost something valuable. What Full-Service does so well, and has done for so many years, deserves to continue. I truly hope that it will.

Bibliography

Books

Barnouw, Eric. *A Tower in Babel: The History of Broadcasting, Part I*. New York: Oxford University Press, 1966.

—. *The Golden Web: The History of Broadcasting, Part II*. New York: Oxford University Press, 1968.

—. *The Image Empire: The History of Broadcasting, Part III*. New York: Oxford University Press, 1970.

Baulu, Roger. *CKAC: Une Histoire d'Amour,* Montreal: Stanké, 1982.

Birkby, Robert. *KMA: The First Sixty Years,* Shenandoah, Iowa: May Broadcasting Company, 1985.

CBC: A Brief History of the Canadian Broadcasting Corporation. Ottawa: CBC, 1976.

Douglas, George H. *The Early Days of Radio Broadcasting*. Jefferson, N.C.: McFarland Press, 1987.

Douglas, Susan J. *Inventing American Broadcasting, 1899–1922*. Baltimore: Johns Hopkins University Press, 1988.

Fowler, Gene, and Bill Crawford. *Border Radio*. Austin: Texas Monthly Press, 1987.

Frith, Simon (ed.). *Facing the Music*. New York: Pantheon, 1988.

Haeg, Jr., Larry. *Sixty Years Strong: The WCCO Story*. Minneapolis: WCCO Press, 1984.

Julian, Joseph. *This Was Radio*. New York: Viking Press, 1975.

Parikhal, John, and David Oakes. *Programming to Win in the New America*. Washington, D.C.: National Association of Broadcasters, 1989.

Poindexter, Ray. *Golden Throats and Silver Tongues: The Radio Announcers*. Little Rock: River Road Press. 1978.

Ries, Al, and Jack Trout. *Positioning: The Battle for Your Mind*. New York: McGraw-Hill, 1986.

Shaw, Arnold. *The Rockin' 50's*. New York: Hawthorn, 1974.

—. *Dictionary of American Pop/Rock*. New York: Macmillan, 1982.

Smith, V. Jackson. *Programming for Radio and Television*. Washington, D.C.: University Press of America, 1983.

Smith Wes, *The Pied Pipers of Rock n' Roll: Radio Deejays of the 50's and 60's*. Marietta, Ga.: Longstreet Press, 1989.

Soloman, Barbara H. (ed.) *Ain't We Got Fun*. New York: New American Library, 1980.

Sterling, Christopher H., and John M. Kittross. *Stay Tuned: A Concise History of American Broadcasting*. Culver City, Cal.: Wadsworth, 1978.

Taylor, Sherril W. (ed.) *Radio Programming in Action.* New York: Hastings House, 1967.

Welcome South, Brother: 50 Years of Broadcasting at WSB. Atlanta: Cox Broadcasting, 1974.

Booklets

Reymer & Gersin. *Radio Wars: How to Survive in the 80's.* Washington D.C.: National Association of Broadcasters, 1983.

—. *Radio Wars II: How to Push Listener Hot Buttons.* Washington, D.C.: National Association of Broadcasters, 1985.

Encyclopedias

Encyclopedia Americana. New York: Grolier, 1986. pp. 150–154.
Canadien Encyclopedia. Edmonton: Hurtig, 1988. pp. 1817–1820.
Colliers Encyclopedia. New York: Macmillan, 1986. pp. 602–603.

Unpublished Doctoral Dissertations

Linton, Bruce, "History of Chicago Radio Station Programming, 1921–1931," Chicago: Northwestern University, 1953.

Locally Produced Pamphlets and Monographs

Brackmann, Charles, and Legette Blythe. "The Hornet's Nest." Public Library of Charlotte, 1961.

Garrett, Franklin M. "Atlanta and Environs: A Chronicle of Its People and Events, Vol. II." Athens: University of Georgia Press, 1969.

"It Started Hear: The History of KDKA Radio." Pittsburgh: KDKA Radio, 1970.

Ross, K. D. "The Birth of a Station: WOWO." Fort Wayne, 1981.

"WTIC: Radio To Remember." Hartford: WTIC Radio, 1985.

Unpublished Magazine Articles

Price, John, "WLW: The Nation's Station." Richmond, Indiana, 1979.

Newspaper Articles

Hanson, Gordon, "KOTA's Early Days Recalled on 50th Anniversary." *Rapid City Journal,* November 26, 1986.

Kinosian, Mike. "WBZ Keeps Boston Buzzing." Los Angeles: *Radio & Records,* March 31, 1989.

—. "Community Involvement and KMOX." Los Angeles: *Radio & Records,* September 16, 1988.

Leininger, Kevin. "WOWO Brightest When Radio Was King." Fort Wayne: *News-Sentinel,* July 10, 1982.

McNutt, Randy, "WLW's Gary Burbank Has Multiple Personalities." Cincinnati: *Tri-State Sunday Magazine,* November 26, 1989.

Pearson, Howard. "KSL: Radio's Golden Era." Salt Lake City: *Deseret News*, April 29, 1972.

"Radio Show Welcomes Home WOC." Davenport, Iowa: *Democrat,* November 9, 1934.

Vagelatos, Alex, "WOWO: Remembering Radio's Days of Old." Fort Wayne: *Journal-Gazette,* December 4, 1987.

Magazine Articles

Couloumbis, Angela. "The Depression and KTSM." *Radio-Active Magazine,* (National Association of Broadcasters), October 1984.

—."Glory Days: Radio's Golden Age Reunion." *Radio-Active Magazine,* September 1985.

"Dean Sorenson: South Dakota's Secret to Small Market Radio." Ft. Lauderdale: *Pulse of Broadcasting Magazine,* November 20, 1989.

Giangola, Andrew. "Marketing AM Radio." New York. *Sound Management Magazine,* May 1986.

Golub, James and Harold Javitz, "Six Ways to Age." *American Demographics,* June 1989.

Halper, Donna L. "All in the Family." *Radio-Active Magazine,* June 1986.

"New AM Formats." Cherry Hill, N.J.: *Radio Only,* October 1986.

Schuster, Joseph. "St. Louis and Sports." *Sport Magazine,* January 1990.

White, Thomas H. "The Mystique of the Three-Letter Call Sign." *DX Monitor Magazine,* February 8, 1986.

Also, I used numerous issues of *Billboard Magazine, Broadcasting, Boston Magazine,* and *Radio-Week* (a National Association of Broadcasters publication). I also used telephone and taped interviews with a number of owners and managers, many of whom are quoted in the book. I again thank them for their cooperation.

```
PN
1991.3   Halper, Donna L.
.U6
H27      Full-service ra-
1991     dio
```

DUE DATE